Words Their Way™

Word Sorts for Within Word Pattern Spellers

Second Edition

Marcia Invernizzi
University of Virginia

Francine Johnston
University of North Carolina, Greensboro

Donald R. Bear
University of Nevada, Reno

Shane Templeton
University of Nevada, Reno

Allyn & Bacon
is an imprint of

PEARSON

Boston   New York   San Francisco
Mexico City   Montreal   Toronto   London   Madrid   Munich   Paris
Hong Kong   Singapore   Tokyo   Cape Town   Sydney

Vice President and Executive Publisher: Jeffery W. Johnston
Senior Editor: Linda Ashe Bishop
Senior Development Editor: Hope Madden
Senior Managing Editor: Pamela D. Bennett
Senior Project Manager: Mary M. Irvin
Editorial Assistant: Demetrius Hall
Senior Art Director: Diane C. Lorenzo
Cover Design: Ali Mohrman
Cover Image: Hope Madden
Operations Specialist: Matthew Ottenweller
Director of Marketing: Quinn Perkson
Marketing Manager: Krista Clark
Marketing Coordinator: Brian Mounts

For related titles and support materials, visit our online catalog at www.pearsonhighered.com

Library of Congress Cataloging in Publication Data

Invernizzi, Marcia.
   Words their way : word sorts for within word pattern spellers / Marcia Invernizzi ... [et al.].—2nd ed.
    p.cm.
   Includes bibliographical references and index.
   ISBN–13: 978-0-13-514843-3
1. English language—Orthography and
spelling—Problems, exercises, etc. I. Title.
   PE1145.2.I58 2009
   428.1'3—dc22

2008002468

Printed in the United States of America

10 9 8 7 6   [BRR]   12 11 10

Allyn & Bacon
is an imprint of

Contents

Overview

Word Sorts for Within Word Pattern Spellers is a companion volume to the core text *Words Their Way: Word Study for Phonics, Vocabulary, and Spelling Instruction* (WTW). The core text supplies the theory and research that underlie the curriculum laid out in these companions and it is important that teachers have this text available for reference.

Within word pattern spellers are typically transitional readers who can identify most one-syllable words in context but still struggle to spell those same words correctly when they write. During this stage of development, students learn to spell long-vowel patterns as well as diphthongs and *r*-influenced vowels. *Words Their Way: Word Sorts for Within Word Pattern Spellers* provides teachers with prepared reproducible sorts and step-by-step directions on how to guide students through sorting lessons. There are organizational tips as well as follow-up activities to extend the lesson through weekly routines. The materials provided in this text will complement the use of any existing phonics, spelling, and reading curricula.

These students are usually in the late first to mid-fourth grades and should already know how to hear and spell two-letter consonant blends and digraphs, as well as short vowels, to be ready for the features in this book. To figure out exactly where individual students should start within this supplement, you need to administer one of the spelling inventories and use the feature guides in Chapter 2 of *WTW*.

Word study as we describe it is analytic. Students examine words they already know how to read, and sometimes even spell, as a way to gain insight into how the spelling system works. This in turn enables them to analyze unfamiliar words they encounter in reading and to master the spelling of similar words. For this reason we do not recommend that you give a pretest and then eliminate all the correctly spelled words from the weekly routines and the final assessment. Known words provide important reference points for the student who is using but confusing the spelling feature of interest. In this way we help students work from the known to the unknown through the scaffolding process.

SCOPE AND SEQUENCE OF THIS BOOK

Research shows that students are using but confusing a variety of vowel patterns at about the same time, so there is some interplay in the sequence presented here among the vowels. Short- and long-vowel sounds are introduced first with pictures, and then the common and less common patterns are introduced. These sorts will include homophones—words that sound the same but are spelled with different patterns to reflect different meanings (e.g., *pair* and *pear*). Students then focus on *r*-influenced vowels, vowel diphthongs, and other ambiguous vowel patterns that reflect a range of vowel sounds that are neither long nor short. Complex consonant patterns such as the *tch* in the word *match* and other consonant patterns that are influenced by vowel sounds are examined in sorts that build on concepts developed in the earlier sorts. At the same time, we expand the repertoire of consonant clusters to include more difficult three-letter digraphs and blends. Silent consonants found at the beginning of words are introduced at this time as well. We start examining two-syllable words toward the end of this sequence by studying two-syllable high-frequency words. Finally, there is a brief introduction to inflectional word endings with the past-tense morpheme (-*ed*) and plurals. The grand finale of this book of sorts is a review of all the long-vowel patterns through the study of homophones.

RESOURCES

For each unit, *Notes for the Teacher* provide placement guidelines and background information about the features of study. The notes also describe weekly routines that ensure practice and enrichment and offer suggestions for books and games. Each unit has at least one spell check to assess student learning. For each sort there are directions for how to introduce the sort as well as additional teaching tips. Sorts are presented as black line masters that can be reproduced for every student so that each student can sort their words a number of times. We recommend that you enlarge the sorts about 10% to maximize the paper size. You should also use the masters to prepare a set of pictures and words for modeling. You may want to make a transparency of the sort and cut it apart for use on an overhead or enlarge the words for use in a pocket chart. You can also simply make your own copy to cut apart and use on a desktop or on the floor.

Most of the sorting lessons are described as teacher-directed closed sorts with preestablished categories indicated with headers and key words. For more discovery-oriented lessons you can cut off the headers and encourage your students to establish their own categories in an open sort. Headers might then be given back to label the columns. The Appendix contains a variety of headers that you can use to label your categories. See Chapters 3 and 6 of *WTW* for additional background information, organizational tips, games, and activities. Use the Independent Word Study form in the Appendix of this book for homework.

PLACEMENT AND PACING

This book contains 10 units of study grouped by early, middle, and late designations in the table of contents. Following are general guidelines for placing students, using the inventory results.

> **Early within word pattern spellers** will know short vowels and will be using but confusing silent vowel markers (FLOTE for *float* or BRITE for *bright*). They may earn 0 to 2 points under "long vowels" on the inventory. They will be ready to contrast short and long vowels with pictures and words in Sorts 1 to 18. If students are still missing two or more short vowels or blends and digraphs they will benefit from the sorts offered in *Word Sorts for Letter Name Spellers*.
>
> **Middle within word pattern spellers** will earn several points under "long vowels" (3 or 4) and may even earn points under "other vowels." They will benefit from the review of common long-vowel patterns and the introduction to less common vowels in Sorts 19 to 30.
>
> **Late within word pattern spellers** will spell most long vowels correctly (missing no more than one on the inventory) but will still make errors in the "other vowel" category. They might take a step back to review *r*-influenced vowels (Sorts 25 to 30) before moving into Sorts 31 to 50.

Each unit contains Spell Checks that can be used as pretests to gather more in-depth information about features and to place your students more accurately. For example, you might give Spell Check 2 (page 32) to students who are in the early within word pattern stage to determine if they can spell words with the common CVCe pattern. If students spell 90% on a spell check correctly, you can safely move on to the next feature. If students spell between 50% and 75% of the words correctly on the pretest, the words and features are at their instructional level.

The pacing for these sorts is designed for slow to average growth and the words selected for the sorts are the most frequently occurring words for that sound or pattern, but feel free to substitute similar words. After introducing a sort, you should spend about a week following routines that encourage students to practice for mastery. If your students seem to be catching on quickly, you can increase the pace by spending fewer days on a sort or you may skip some sorts altogether. On the other hand, you may need to slow down and perhaps even create additional sorts for some students using the blank template in the Appendix. Additional words are included for most sorts to provide more practice or to challenge students with a more developed reading vocabulary. Additional sorts and words may be found in the Appendix of *WTW* as well as on the CD-ROM.

ENGLISH LANGUAGE LEARNERS

Many of the vowel sounds in English do not exist in other languages, and the sounds that are the same may be spelled with different letters. For example, the Spanish language has only one short-vowel sound (short -*o* spelled with *a*), one diphthong (*oi*) and no *r*-influenced vowels. Long -*o* and long -*u* are spelled with those corresponding letters, but the long -*a* sound is spelled with *e*, long -*e* with *i*, and long -*i* with *ai*. If students are literate in their first language, they may try to spell the sounds they hear in English with the correspondences they know from their first language. Word sorting lessons will help them sort out the differences and focus their attention on new sounds and patterns, but expect English Language Learners (ELLs) to need extra practice and support. Following are several suggestions.

1. Reduce the number of words in a sort.
2. Spend extra time saying the words aloud and discussing meanings, not only in the introductory lesson but also throughout the week.
3. Pair ELLs with English speakers for partner work.
4. Accept variations in pronunciation. (Even native English speakers pronounce vowel sounds in a variety of ways.) Allow students to sort in ways that make sense to them but still reflect sound and pattern correspondences. For example, students may sort the words *mail*, *snail*, and *pail* separately from *rain*, *paid*, and *paint*, but the *-ail* words fall into their own pattern category.

Unit 1 Picture Sorts for Short- and Long-Vowel Sounds

NOTES FOR THE TEACHER

Background and Objectives

These first six picture sorts are designed to focus students' attention on the vowel sound in the middle of single-syllable words and to provide ample practice in recognizing, identifying, and categorizing vowel sounds as either long or short. Direct instruction in segmenting and isolating the vowel sound in the middle of single-syllable words lays the phonological foundation for learning how to spell long-vowel patterns. Students will:

- Segment and identify the medial vowels in pictured words
- Review short-vowel correspondences and learn that long vowels "say their names"

Targeted Learners

Some students should begin their study of long-vowel patterns by comparing and contrasting short- and long-vowel sounds in single-syllable words. Directly teaching vowel sounds with pictures is especially useful for students in the very early within word pattern stage. Typically these children are in late first or second grade. The first six picture sorts can be used with students who have mastered the spelling of most two-letter consonant digraphs and blends at the beginning and end of words and correctly represent most short-vowel sounds in the middle. If you see that students are selecting the correct short and long vowels but simply omitting the silent long vowel markers (HOP for *hope* or BRIT for *bright*), then you will want to skip to later sorts in this book. You may also want to use Spell Check 1 for a pretest to see which students will require instruction in isolating the medial vowel sound.

Teaching Tips

These sorts can be used a number of ways depending on the needs of your students and the pace you set. You may want to use these sorts sequentially with lots of repeated practice in first grade or with students who struggle to hear the difference in vowel sounds. You may just want to use Sort 6 to introduce the idea of long vowels and the five long-vowel sounds. You may want to use each sort to introduce Sorts 7 to 12. For example, you might use the pictures in Sort 1 to focus attention on the sounds of long and short *-a* one day, and then have students sort words using Sort 7 the next day.

Some students may think that the terms *long* and *short* refer to the height or length of the letters on the page. Be sure they understand that the term *long vowel* refers to the *sound* of the vowel. The sound is really not any longer than a short vowel but these are the terms that are most familiar to teachers and students. When students know the terms it is easier to talk about the discoveries they make in the word sorts.

The pictures in Sorts 1 to 6 represent words that are already in most students' oral vocabulary. English Language Learners (ELLs) may learn new words by working collaboratively with a buddy who names each picture as it is sorted. Key pictures that highlight the vowel under study are provided to associate with each sound and these should be placed at the top of each column to explicitly label the category. These same headers will be used in Sorts 7 to 12 and are also used on the sound board found in the Appendix of *WTW*. Briefly point out to students how the vowels are marked to indicate short and long sounds. You do not have to use the terms *breve* and *macron*, but students will see these symbols often and should know that they stand for sounds.

Five picture sorts in this section feature one-syllable words for each of the five vowels. Each sort also contains an oddball (e.g., *foot* in Sort 1). Sort 6 contrasts the long-vowel sounds of all five vowels. Because these six introductory sorts are so similar, you may be able to introduce and practice three picture sorts per week. While working with picture sorts, children will practice phoneme segmentation skills as they learn to divide each word into its individual sounds. Students who find it difficult to isolate the medial vowel sound will need a slower, more explicit presentation. When phoneme segmentation is difficult, students should be encouraged to peel away the consonant sounds at the beginning and end of the word to isolate the vowel sound in the middle. For example, if students are having difficulty segmenting the word *rain* into three individual phonemes, try having them say *rain* without the /r/ sound (*ain*); and then *ain* without the /n/ sound. To make these sorts even more explicit, ask students to segment and count the individual sounds within a few words in each category. For example, after sorting the picture of the *slide* under the key picture/word for the long *-i* sound (*kite*), you may ask students to count the four sounds in the word *slide*, perhaps by pushing a counter for each sound. After deconstructing the sounds within the word, students should blend the sounds together again to reconstruct it (e.g., /s/ + /l/ + /i/ + /d/ = *slide*).

Literature Connection

When possible, share books that contain a number of words with the same vowel sounds being studied. For example, *Jake Baked the Cake* (Hennessy, 1992) is a natural connection to the long *-a* sound, whereas *Sheep in a Jeep* (Shaw, 1997) plays on the long *-e*. You may also have poems, rhymes, or traditional chants that feature short- and long-vowel sounds, such as *Old Hogan's Goat* in *Juba This and Juba That* (Tashjian, 1969). You might present these on a chart or overhead and underline target words before or after doing the sorting activities.

Standard Weekly Routines for Use with Picture Sorts 1–6

1. *Repeated Work with the Pictures.*   Students should repeat the sort several times after it has been modeled and discussed under the teacher's direction. After cutting out the pictures and using them for individual practice, the pieces can be stored in an envelope or baggie to sort again several times on other days. See *WTW* (Chapter 3) for tips on managing picture sorting.

2. *Draw and Label and Cut and Paste.*   For seat work, students can draw additional pictures of words containing the targeted vowel sounds. They can also look for pictures in magazines and catalogs and paste those into categories according to the medial vowel sound. The pictures from the black line sort can be pasted into categories

and children can be asked to label them. This can serve as an assessment tool but *do not* expect accurate spelling of the entire word at this time.

3. *Games and Other Activities.*   Many games are described in *WTW* and are available to print out from the *WTW* CD-ROM. Variations of the Follow-the-Path game work especially well for short- and long-vowel sounds. You might want to create one with all five long vowels.

SORTS 1-6   SHORT- AND LONG-VOWEL SOUNDS

Demonstrate, Sort, Check, and Reflect

(See page 10.)

1. Prepare a set of pictures to use for teacher-directed modeling. Use the key pictures as headers and display the pictures randomly, picture side up.

2. Begin a sound sort by modeling one picture into each column, **demonstrating** and explaining explicitly what you are doing. Model by stretching out the vowel sound in the middle to emphasize its sound: *Here is a picture of rain . . . Rrr—aaaa—nn; I hear the letter A say its name in the middle. When we hear a vowel say its name in the middle, we call it a long-vowel sound. I hear a long -a in the middle of rain, so I will put it under the picture of the cake. This is a picture of a bag. Bb—aaa—gg has a short -a in the middle—the /a/ sound like in the middle of the word* cat. *I'll put* bag *under* cat *because they both have the /a/ sound, the short -a sound in the middle. Now who can help me sort the rest of these pictures?* Model several more and then continue with the children's help to **sort** all of the pictures. Be sure to model the discovery and placement of the oddball. Say something like this: *Listen to the sound in the middle of* foot. */fooooot/. Does that have the sounds we are listening for today? It's an oddball because it does not have either the long or short -a sound so we will put it over here by itself.* When all the pictures have been sorted, **check** the sort by naming all of the pictures in each column to make sure they all have the same vowel sound in the middle. *Do all of these sound alike in the middle? Do we need to move any?*

3. Repeat the sort with the group again. Keep the key pictures and the letter as headers and take some time to explicitly talk about the way the vowels are marked short with a curve ˘ or long with a straight line ¯. You may want to mix up the pictures and turn them face down in a deck this time and let children take turns drawing a card and sorting it in the correct column. You can also simply pass out the pictures and have the children take turns sorting them. After sorting, model how to check by naming the words in each column and then **reflect**. Talk about how the words in each column are alike and how they are different from the words in the other column. Review the oddballs or any other words that were difficult to categorize and explain why.

Extend

Give each student a copy of the sort for individual practice or let students work with partners if they need support in naming the pictures. Enlarge the sort sheet by 10% before copying to eliminate the border. Before the students cut apart the pictures, have them individualize their sheet by using different colors of crayon to scribble over or draw lines down the back of their paper. Then assign the students to sort on their own in the same way they did in the group. As they sort independently, ask individual students about how they are sorting and why they placed a particular picture in a column. Ask them to tell you what sounds they are working on. Give each student a plastic bag or envelope to store the pieces. On subsequent days students should repeat the sorting activity several times. Involve the students in the other weekly routines listed above and described in *WTW* for the within word pattern stage. The *WTW* CD-ROM has additional picture sorts with matching words that work with these same sounds.

Sort 1

ă and cat		ā and cake		oddball
crab	flag	skate	plate	foot
map	man	frame	chain	
hat		shave	game	
bat		rain	rake	
bag		snail	snake	
grass		grapes		

Sort 2

ĭ and pig		ī and kite		oddball
fish	zip	pie	dive	net
lid		drive	fire	
lips		slide	vine	
hill		hive	five	
twins		nine	prize	
swim		smile	bride	

Sort 3

ŏ and sock		ō and bone		oddball
rock	clock	smoke	ghost	web
mop	box	toes	coat	
dot		road	soap	
lock		nose	hose	
fox		robe	boat	
top		goat		

Sort 4

ŭ and cup		ū and tube		oddball
rug	plug	glue	shoe	skate
thumb	sun	suit	flute	
tub	drum	spoon	fruit	
bug	gum	mule	roof	
truck	nut	moon		

Sort 5

ĕ and bed		ē and feet		oddball
sled	leg	peas	tree	fork
vest		deer	jeep	
bell		cheese	wheel	
dress		seal	queen	
desk		sheep	sleep	
nest		sweep		

Sort 6 Pictures and Words

long *a* and cake	long *e* and feet	long *i* and kite	long *o* and bone	long *u* and tube
tape	bee	bike	cone	cube
cane	tree	bride	rose	flute
snake				

Notes for Sort 6: Sort 6 provides a review of all five long vowels and can be used to transition to the next set of sorts where students will sort just words. Lay down the headers for each long-vowel sound and talk about the medial vowel sound and the symbol used to represent that sound. Then sort the pictures by the vowel sounds in the middle. After checking the placement of the pictures, match each word card to its corresponding picture. Talk about the fact that there is a silent *e* at the end of each word that cannot be heard.

SPELL CHECK 1   ASSESSMENT FOR MEDIAL LONG-VOWEL SOUNDS

(See page 16.) Spell Check 1 can be used as a pretest and/or posttest to determine if students can isolate and identify the medial long vowels. For students who have full phonemic awareness, this should be an easy task because the long vowels "say their names." Name each picture and ask students to circle the vowel they hear in the middle of the word. Students who score 10 or better can move on to the next set of sorts. The words are:

1. kite	**2.** leaf	**3.** rope	**4.** suit
5. rain	**6.** slide	**7.** soap	**8.** peach
9. gate	**10.** feet	**11.** paint	**12.** fruit

SORT 1   Picture Sort for Long and Short -a

ă 🐱	ā 🥫	oddball	

SORT 2   Picture Sort for Long and Short -i

ĭ 🐷	ī 🪁	oddball	

SORT 3   Picture Sort for Long and Short -o

ō 🦴	ŏ 🧦	oddball	

SORT 4   Picture Sort for Long and Short -u

ŭ 🍵	ū 🧦	oddball	

SORT 5   Picture Sort for Long and Short -*e*

ĕ 🛏	ē 🦶	oddball	

SORT 6   Review of Long-Vowels with Word Matches

ā cake	ē feet	ī kite	ō bone
ū tube	tape	bike	cone
cube	bee	cane	bride
rose	flute	tree	snake

Spell Check 1   Long-Vowels

Name _____

a e i o u	a e i o u	a e i o u
a e i o u	a e i o u	a e i o u
a e i o u	a e i o u	a e i o u
a e i o u	a e i o u	a e i o u

Unit II   Word Sorts Contrasting Short- and Long-Vowel Sounds and Patterns (CVC and CVCe)

NOTES FOR THE TEACHER

Background and Objectives

The silent *e*, or CVCe pattern, is the most common long-vowel spelling for long *a, i, o,* and *u*. Most students easily notice that the addition of the silent *e* changes the short-vowel sound into a long-vowel sound that says its name: *tap* becomes *tape; can* becomes *cane; cub* becomes *cube*. In single-syllable words, the CVCe pattern does not occur often for *e*, so the long-vowel spellings of *e* are not included here. The few CVCe words for *e* may be found in the next set of sorts (13 to 18) that examine other long-vowel patterns. Students will:

- Learn to distinguish the short- and long-vowel sounds for *a, i, o* and *u*
- Learn to use the CVCe pattern to spell the long-vowel sounds in targeted words
- Learn when to use the final *-ck, -ke,* and *-k* spellings

Targeted Learners

Sorts 7 to 12 are designed for students in the early within word pattern stage who are starting to use but still confuse the final silent *e*. Most of the words in these sorts are on a late first- and second-grade level and it is important that your students can read the words before trying to sort them. More difficult words that follow the same pattern are also provided with each sort for more advanced readers. You might use Spell Check 2 on page 32 as a pretest to see which of your students are in need of these particular sorts. Students who spell most of the words (90%) on the Spell Check correctly may benefit from the study of other common long-vowel patterns in the next section.

Teaching Tips

Although you want your students to use spelling patterns to help them read and spell, you do not want them to overrely on visual cues to the exclusion of the sound they represent. The silent *e* at the end of words proffers a strong visual pull. In Sorts 7 to 12 we take several measures to offset the visual. First, we include several pictures with each word sort in this section to induce students to categorize by sound as well as by pattern. Second, we recommend the use of blind or no-peeking sorts as a standard weekly routine, because these sorts require students to categorize a word by sound before they consider its spelling pattern. These and other weekly routines are described in Chapters 3 and 6 of *WTW*. Third, we incorporate oddballs that violate the prevailing pattern-to-sound correspondence. High-frequency words like *come, some, done,* and *have* are oddballs that will keep your students on their toes. These words are spelled with the CVCe pattern but do not have the long-vowel sound. Students should be encouraged to find "the odd one out" after they sort and to articulate why it does not fit into either category by sound or pattern. You may want to use the picture sorts in the previous unit to introduce or to extend the word sorts in this unit. The same key words and pictures that were used to head the categories in Sorts 1 to 6 are used again here. Sort 11 is a review that requires students to categorize short- and long-vowel sounds and patterns across all four vowels. Sort 12 focuses on the spelling of words ending in *-ck, -ke,* or *-k,* and demonstrates how these word endings are also tied directly to the vowel sounds.

English Language Learners may find it easier to identify the long vowels in these sorts than the short vowels, especially students whose home language is Spanish. In this case, these sorts will serve as a review of the short vowel and the contrast will help them sort out the differences in sound and letter correspondences.

Literature Connection

Use books for instruction that feature a number of words with a targeted feature so that children will see these words in the context of reading and have the opportunity to practice them. Many publishers are creating phonics readers or decodable text that can complement the study of vowels, but look for books that students can read with at least 90% accuracy. Phyllis Trachtenburg created a list of trade books by phonics features that you can find online (search by "Trachtenburg and trade books") or refer to the original article in *The Reading Teacher* (May 1990). *Make Way for Ducklings* (McCloskey, 1941) is a natural connection for the *-ck* versus *-ke* and *-k* distinctions presented in Sort 12 because the ducklings' names are Jack, Kack, Lack, Mack, Nack, Ouack, Pack, and Quack. You may also have poems or chants that feature similar short- and long-vowel sounds and patterns, such as *Seven Little Rabbits* (Tashijian, 1941), that feature many long-vowel sounds. You might present these on a chart or overhead and underline target words before or after doing the sorting and activities.

Standard Weekly Routines for Within Word Pattern Spellers*

1. *Repeated Work with the Sort.*   Make a copy of the sort for each student so they can work individually with the featured sorts several times after the sort has been modeled and discussed in the group. Have students scribble on the back of their handout in different colors to identify their words and then cut it apart. The pieces can be stored in an envelope or plastic bag to be sorted again on other days of the week. Extra sorting can also be done for homework and a special homework form is supplied in the Appendix.

2. *Writing Sorts and Word Study Notebooks.*   Students should record their word sorts by writing them into columns in their notebooks under the key words established in the group sort. Writing helps secure the spelling of words in memory as students make decisions about the correct categories and provides a "home base" for the other weekly routines and homework assignments. At the bottom of the writing sort, have your students **reflect** on what they learned in that particular sort and write their observations about the spelling of certain sounds. Students may be asked to select some words to illustrate or to use some of them (not *all* of them) in sentences to demonstrate the meaning of the words. This is especially valuable for words with multiple meanings and for homophones.

*See Chapters 3 and 6 of *WTW* for more detailed information about these and other word study routines.

3. *Blind Sorts and Writing Sorts.*   A blind or no-peeking sort should only be done after students have had a chance to practice a word sort several times, but it is critically important if students are to learn the spelling patterns that go with partic- ular words. Key words are laid down as headers. Students work with a partner who calls out a word without showing it. The other student points to where the word should go and the partner lays down the word card to check its spelling against the key word. In a blind or no-peeking writing sort, key words are written at the top of a sheet of paper. The student then writes the words in the correct column as they are called aloud. After the word has been written, the partner calling the words imme- diately shows the word card to the student doing the writing to check for correct- ness. Blind sorts require students to think about words by sound and by pattern and to use the key words as models for analogy. They are a great way to practice for spelling tests and can be assigned for homework.

4. *Word Hunts.*   Students can look for words in stories and poems that mirror the featured sound or pattern. These words should then be added to the proper column in their word study notebook. Encourage students to find the same sounds and patterns in two-syllable words such as the *-ay* in the final syllable of *delay*. You may want to create posters or displays of all the words students can discover for each category.

5. *Word-O or Word-Operations.*   This activity is especially appropriate for early within word pattern spellers. Model for students how they can change one letter in a word to make a new word. Typically, consonants, blends, and digraphs are exchanged for other consonants at the beginning (*make-bake-brake-rake-lake-flake*) or end (*mad-mat- math-mash-mask*) of words. As students progress further through this stage, see if they can change the vowel in the middle to create a new word (*drive-drove; give-gave*). Give students four to six words at a time to work with and challenge them to see how many words they can create. Students can record their word operations in their word study notebooks.

6. *Homophone Collection.*   Homophones turn up frequently in these sorts and it is fun to create an ongoing record that will grow across the entire year. This might be in the form of a group chart or "Pair/Pear Tree" displayed on a bulletin board. Some teach- ers create a class homophone book and students take turns adding new words, pictures, and sentences to illustrate the book. Students can keep their own collection in a special section of their word study notebook.

7. *Speed Sorts.*   Using a stopwatch, students time themselves as they sort their words into categories. After obtaining a baseline speed, students repeat the sort several times and try to beat their own time. Repeated, timed speed sorts help students internalize spelling patterns and become automatic in recognizing them.

8. *Games and Other Activities.*   Create games and activities such as those in *WTW* or download them ready made from the *WTW* CD-ROM. The Train Station game and the Race Track game are highly recommended for use with all vowel patterns. Other games, such as Turkey Feathers, Vowel Poker, Word Study Pursuit, and UNO, are described in Chapter 6. Scattergories can be found on the *WTW* CD-ROM of the 4th edition.

9. *Assessment.*   To assess students' mastery, ask them to spell the words using a traditional end-of-the-week spelling test format. We recommend that you call out 10 to 12 of the words instead of the whole list. You might also prepare a sen- tence that contains several words. Read the sentence to your students and have them write it. Give them feedback about their spelling and mechanics. Spell Checks are provided for each unit in this book and can be used as both a pretest and posttest.

SORT 7   SHORT -*A* VERSUS LONG -*A* IN CVCe

(See page 26.) Prepare a set of pictures and words to use for teacher-directed modeling. Read over the words and discuss any that are unfamiliar. Students should be able to read all the words, but if not, give them extra support identifying the words until they can name them idependently with repeated exposure. Feel free to discard troublesome words. Ask your students if they notice anything about the words (they all have an *a* in them). Ask about the vowel sounds in the middle of the words. Do they all have the same vowel sound? Students might cut their own sets of words in advance to bring to the group.

Demonstrate

Introduce the short -*a* symbol and the long -*a* symbol on the headers and say each key word slowly to model the phoneme segmentation process involved in isolating and identifying each vowel sound: *Listen to the short* -a *sound in* cat: *caaaat, aaaa. Listen to the long* -a *sound in* cake: *caaaaake aaaaa.* Be sure to include the oddball header for words that do not fit the other two categories. Explain that they will say each word and compare it to the key words to sort them into a column: *Here is the word* mad. *Listen to the vowel sound in the middle and compare it to our two key words:* mad-cat *or* mad-cake? *We will put the word* mad *under* cat *because they have the same short vowel sound.* Have your students join in as you continue to model the isolation, identification, and categorization of the medial vowel sound. After sorting a few, be sure to model the word *what* and how to decide when a word does not fit either category. Explain why *what* is an oddball; *what* is spelled like it should have a short -*a* sound but it does not: The middle sound of *what* sounds like /uh/ instead of the short -*a* sound. When you are finished sorting, read the words down in each column and ask the students how they are alike and how they are different from the other words. Ask them what they notice about the way the words are spelled and lead them to talk about how the long -*a* words end with a silent *e* and the short -*a* words do not.

Sort

Have your students shuffle their cards and sort them in the same way. Remember to have them head up their categories with the same key words and pictures that you used, including the oddball header. Tell your students to say each word aloud as they sort. The final sort should look like this (pictures are in brackets):

Short -*a* [cat]		Long -*a* [cake]		oddball
last*	ask	make*	page	what*
[glass]	grass	face	rake	
fast	hand*	same	came*	
snap	mad	[gate]	[whale]	
sack	[bat]	name*	made*	

*High-frequency word

Check

After the students sort, have them check their own sorts by reading each word and picture in a column to make sure they all sound the same in the middle. If a student does not notice a mistake, guide him or her to it by saying: *One of these doesn't fit. See if you can hear which one as I read them all.* Then read each word card, being careful to enunciate each vowel sound clearly. If the student still does not hear the oddball, read through the column again, then revisit the misplaced word and compare it to each key word and symbol. Ask the student which column the word should go in and why.

Reflect

After checking the sort, ask your students to reflect on their sort and declare their categories by sound and pattern. You might model how to write a reflection such as: *Words with short* -a *have only one vowel in the middle and words with long* -a *have a silent* e *on the end.* After modeling this process a few times you can begin to expect them to do this on their own.

Extend

Have students store their words and pictures in an envelope or plastic bag so they can reuse them throughout the week in individual and buddy sorts. Introduce blind or no-peeking sorts after students have repeated the sort several times. See the list of standard weekly routines for follow-up activities to the basic sorting lesson. To provide more practice sorting by sound either before or after Sort 7, you can use Sort 1 which is only pictures.

Additional Words.   *fact, sand, bath, math, swam, chat, class, tame, fake, wade, grape, flame, scale, fame, lane, whale, blame, blaze, skate, was, saw* (oddballs)

SORT 8   SHORT -*I* VERSUS LONG -*I* IN CVCe

(See page 27.) Prepare a set of pictures and words to use for teacher-directed modeling as described in Sort 7. Read and discuss any unfamiliar words. Ask your students what they notice about the spelling of the words in the sort.

Demonstrate

Introduce the short -*i* and the long -*i* symbols on the headers and model how to isolate the sounds in the key words. Review the oddball header for words that do not have the other two sounds. Tell your students that they will compare and contrast the spelling patterns of short and long -*i* words. Demonstrate the sorting process by saying the word and comparing it to each key word, picture, and symbol. Have your students join in as you continue to model the isolation, identification, and categorization of the medial vowel sound. After you have sorted a few, hold up the word *give* and ask where the word might belong. When you are finished demonstrating the sort, ask your students how the words in each column are alike and how they are different. Help to focus their attention on the pattern and the fact that long -*i* words have an *e* at the end. Revisit the oddball *give* and help them see that it is spelled like a long -*i* word—it has a silent *e* on the end—but the vowel sound in the middle of *give* is short.

   Have your students shuffle their cards and sort them using the same headers. Have your students say each word aloud as they sort. The final sort should look like this (pictures are in brackets):

Short -*i* [pig]		Long -*i* [kite]		oddball
swim	gift	five*	nice	give*
rich	[clip]	drive	while*	
[stick]	spill	mice	[knife]	
thin	[kick]	[dice]	nine	
flip	dish	hike	prize	

*High-frequency word

Check

After the students sort, have them check their own sorts by reading each word and picture in a column to make sure they all sound the same in the middle and all have the same spelling pattern.

Reflect

After checking the sort, ask your students to reflect on their sort and declare their categories by sound and pattern. You can ask your students to mark the long and short vowels in the key words using macrons and breves and students can write a summary of what they learned about spelling short -*i* and long -*i* words in their word study notebooks.

Extend

Have students store their words and pictures in an envelope or plastic bag so they can reuse them in individual and buddy sorts. Students should repeat this sort several times throughout the week. Use the standard weekly routines for follow-up activities to this basic sorting lesson. Because students will be able to sort visually by just looking at the final *e*, it is especially important to include blind or no-peeking sorts.

Additional Words.   *slid, grin, skip, grip, fifth, skill, shine, glide, pride, spine, tribe, ripe, pine, price, file, drive, life, hive, smile, while, climb* (oddball).

SORT 9   SHORT -*O* VERSUS LONG -*O* IN CVCe

(See page 28.) Introduce this sort in a manner similar to that described for Sorts 7 and 8. As you read and discuss the words, be sure to talk about the meanings of the word *hole* so that students do not confuse it with *whole*. The word *hose* has several meanings (a garden hose for water and hose you might wear). The words *come* and *some* are oddballs in this sort because they have the CVCe spelling pattern but do not have the long -*o* sound. Conduct this sort using the same lesson format: **Demonstrate, sort, check, reflect,** and **extend.** The sort will end up looking something like this (pictures are in brackets):

Short -*o* [sock]		Long -*o* [bone]		oddball
rock	[pot]	home	joke	come*
job	chop	stove	nose	some*
hot	[clock]	hose	broke	
spot		[cone]	woke	
		hope	hole	
		those	[rope]	

*High-frequency word

Additional Words.   *flock, plot, flop, slot, plop, clog, lone, pole, mole, tone, vote, robe, role, choke, stole, once, dove* (oddballs)

SORT 10   SHORT -*U* VERSUS LONG -*U* IN CVCe

(See page 29.) Introduce the sort in a manner similar to Sorts 7 and 8. The word *put* is an oddball because it is pronounced as if it rhymes with *foot* instead of *cut*. Note: There is a slight difference in the long -*u* sound in *use* and *cute* (where the vowel says its name y͞oo) and in *tune* and *flute* (o͞o). Children may or may not notice this difference. Either way, the sound is spelled the same.

Demonstrate, Sort, Check, Reflect, and Extend

Demonstrate, sort, check, reflect, and **extend.** The sort will look something like this (pictures are in brackets):

Short -*u* [cup]		Long -*u* [tube]		oddball
just*	shut	use*	flute	put*
drum	club	huge	[mule]	
[bus]	[cut]	June	cute	
hunt	such*	[cube]	tune	
jump	[plus]	rude	tube	

*High-frequency word

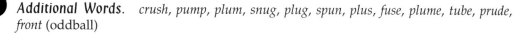

Additional Words.   *crush, pump, plum, snug, plug, spun, plus, fuse, plume, tube, prude, front* (oddball)

SORT 11   SHORT VERSUS LONG REVIEW (CVC AND CVCe)

(See page 30.) Note that the column headers for this sort are different. The column headers label the pattern of consonants and vowels for each vowel sound. The label *CVC* refers to the consonant(s) to the left and right of the short vowel. The label *CVCe* refers to the pattern of consonants and vowels for the long vowel. Read and discuss any unfamiliar words. *Which* might be confused with *witch*. You can introduce the term *homophone* for these words but students will be seeing homophone pairs in the next set of sorts where the idea will become more familiar to them.

Demonstrate, Sort, Check, and Reflect

Introduce headers *CVC-short, CVCe-long,* and *oddball.* Tell your students that they will be comparing and contrasting the short- and long-vowel spellings of all four of the vowels they have been studying in the previous four sorts. Explain that the CVC refers to the consonant-vowel-consonant spelling pattern of the short vowels. Write up several words and label them. *Fat* = CVC, but so is *flat* and *flock*. Label the consonants in *crop* as CCVC and in *which* as CCVCC. Explain that all three words have a short vowel and CVC is used to represent all of them. The CVCe refers to the consonant-vowel-consonant -*e* spelling pattern of the long vowels. Demonstrate the sorting process by saying each word and comparing it to each header. Have your students join you as you model sorting by pattern. See if they can spot the oddballs—the words *done* and *have* contain the CVCe pattern but not the long-vowel sound. When you are finished demonstrating the sort, ask your students how the words in each column are alike by sound and by pattern. Reflect as a group on the pattern-to-sound consistency in the CVC and CVCe patterns across all four vowels.

The ubiquitous silent *e* at the end of so many words may tempt some students to sort by pattern alone. They may categorize all of the words with an *e* at the end into one group together. However, the words *done* and *have* will no doubt be misplaced. If this is the case, ask your students to read all of the words in a column aloud to make sure they all have the same sound.

CVC short		CVCe long		oddball
which*	drip	these*	cape	done
wax	crop	mule	tide	have*
skin		rule	vote	
crab		note	wipe	
lots		safe	race	
gum		wife		

*High-frequency word

Extend

See the list of standard weekly routines. At this point you can also **review** all four long vowels using pictures and words from Sorts 7, 8, 9, and 10. Challenge students to sort into four categories. You might try this with just the words by creating your own word sort sheet using the template in the Appendix. List long-vowel words from all four vowels randomly for students to cut apart and sort by long-vowel sounds. Follow this up with blind or no-peeking sorts where children take turns reading the words for their partner to sort or write.

Additional Words.   *slap, shade, mate, chip, spite, slice, sob, owe, wove, stroke, mast, crate, clip, wide, phone*

SORT 12   FINAL /K/ SOUND SPELLED -*CK*, -*KE*, OR -*K*

(See page 31.) Students in the within word pattern stage may overgeneralize the final -*ck* digraph in long-vowel words, spelling the word *smoke*, SMOCKE, for example. Students need to discover that the final /k/ sound in single-syllable words is directly related to the vowel sound that precedes it. These spelling distinctions are tied directly to the vowel sound. In this sort the ambiguous, but common, double *oo* pattern and sound /o͝o/ (as in *look*) is also introduced with words that students are likely to know. This sound is reviewed later and compared to the long -*oo* sound (*hoop*) in Sort 32.

Read and discuss any unfamiliar words. Ask your students if they notice anything about all of the words (they all have *k* in them). You may want to cut off the headers and ask students to do an open sort. Some may sort by pattern, others by sound. Either way the results will be similar.

Demonstrate, Sort, Check, and Reflect

Introduce headers -*ck*, -*ke*, and -*k*. Tell your students that they will be comparing and contrasting the spelling of the final /k/ sound. Demonstrate the sorting process by using the bolded key words: *kick, take,* and *took.* Say each word and compare it to each header. Have your students join you as you continue to model sorting by the spelling of the final /k/ sound at the end of each word. When you are finished demonstrating the sort, ask your students how the words in each column are alike by vowel sound. See if they notice that all of the words ending in -*ck* have short-vowel sounds; all of the words ending in -*ke* have long-vowel sounds; and all of the words ending in -*k* have vowel sounds that are neither long nor short. If your students do not notice this on their own, read the words in each column carefully and tell them directly. At this point you might compare the -*ck* spelling to the CVC pattern of previous sorts and point out that it is still a CVC pattern. Likewise, compare the -*ke* spelling to the CVCe pattern of the previous sort. Read all of the words in the -*k* column aloud and ask the students what they notice about them (they rhyme and they all have the same spelling pattern).

After your demonstration, have the students **sort, check,** and then **reflect** on this sort. Be sure to have them **declare** what spellings go with which vowel sounds. The sort will look something like this:

-*ck*		-*ke*		-*k*	
kick	pack	**take**	duke	**took**	look
sick	lick	bike	strike	shook	book
lock	sock	shake	smoke	cook	
duck	truck	spoke	like		

Extend
See the list of standard weekly routines. You might try dictating a sentence such as: *I took a snack and a book in my pack when I went for a hike.* See also the Take-A-Card game on the *WTW* CD-ROM for more *ck, ke,* and *k* spellings.

Additional Words.   *stack, track, quack, brake, quake, flake, wake, brick, chick, click, spike, poke, clove, pluck, hook, nook*

SPELL CHECK 2   ASSESSMENT FOR SHORT- AND LONG-VOWEL (CVCe) PATTERNS

(See page 32.) The spelling of short vowels following the consonant-vowel-consonant (CVC) pattern and the spelling of long vowels following the consonant-vowel-consonant-silent *e* patterns (CVCe) are assessed with the Spell Check for Short and Long (CVCe). All of the words pictured have been presented previously in Sorts 7 to 12. Name each picture, then ask your students to think about each word's vowel sound and write the spelling of the word on the lines provided. Students can also complete this independently. Following are the 20 words assessed.

1. hose	2. tube	3. duck	4. tape
5. book	6. sack	7. bone	8. kick
9. sock	10. mule	11. bike	12. flute
13. five	14. rock	15. smoke	16. stove
17. rake	18. kite	19. lock	20. cape

SORT 7   Short -a Versus Long -a (CVCe)

ă cat	ā cake	*oddball*
mad		make
fast	hand	what
	snap	last
page	came	
	grass	face
name	rake	ask
same	made	sack

SORT 8   Short -*i* Versus Long -*i* (CVCe)

ĭ 🐖 pig	ī ◇ kite	*oddball*
dish	(image: stick)	five
rich	mice	prize
(image: knife)	gift	hike
while	flip	(image: kick)
(image: paper clip)	thin	swim
nice	drive	spill
nine	give	(image: dice)

SORT 9   Short -o Versus Long -o (CVCe)

ŏ sock	ō bone	*oddball*
rock		nose
job	hope	those
	hot	hose
joke	home	
	come	hole
some	spot	chop
stove	woke	broke

SORT 10   Short -u Versus Long -u (CVCe)

ŭ cup	ū tube	*oddball*
drum		cute
use	huge	just
	jump	hunt
shut	tube	
	tune	such
club	June	rude
flute		put

SORT 11   Short Versus Long Review (CVC and CVCe)

CVC short	CVCe long	*oddball*
which	note	mule
done	wax	rule
these	skin	safe
crab	wife	lots
cape	tide	gum
have	drip	vote
race	crop	wipe

SORT 12   Final /k/ Sound Spelled -ck, -ke, or -k

-ck	-ke	-k
kick	take	took
bike	sick	lock
shook	shake	duck
duke	spoke	pack
strike	cook	lick
sock	smoke	look
truck	like	book

Spell Check 2   Assessment for Short- and Long-Vowel (CVCe) Patterns

Name _____

1. _____

2. _____

3. _____

4. _____

5. _____

6. _____

7. _____

8. _____

9. _____

10. _____

11. _____

12. _____

13. _____

14. _____

15. _____

16. _____

17. _____

18. _____

19. _____

20. _____

Unit III Common Long-Vowel Patterns (CVCe and CVVC)

NOTES FOR THE TEACHER

Background and Objectives

Another common long-vowel pattern is the consonant-vowel-vowel-consonant (CVVC) pattern. Every vowel except the vowel *i* uses this pattern to represent the long-vowel sound. We caution you to avoid teaching your students the old expression, "When two vowels go walking the first one does the talking." It works well with vowel digraphs like *ai*, *oa*, and *ea*, covered in these sorts, but it does not work with pairs like *ou*, *oo*, and *oy*, covered in later units. Although the CVVC pattern is the new long-vowel spelling pattern introduced in this section, the CVC and CVCe of the previous six sorts reappear in new words and provide a starting point for comparison. Because the vowel *i* does not use the CVVC pattern, other vowel patterns for *i* are presented in the next section.

Homophones are common in these long-vowel words so you will want to spend time talking about their meanings. They are italicized in the word lists. High-frequency words (that appear in Frye's top 200) are included in the sorts, some as oddballs. They are marked in the word lists with an asterisk. Students will:

- Review the short-vowel sounds and the CVCe pattern for long vowels
- Learn the CVVC pattern for long vowels (*ai*, *oa*, *oo*, *ui*, *ee*, *ea*) and the *ea* pattern for short *e*

Targeted Learners

Sorts 13 to 18 are designed for early-to-middle within word pattern stage spellers who are using but confusing the CVVC and CVCe patterns. They might spell the word *foam*, FOME; or the word *slope*, SLOAP. Most of the words in these sorts are on a second- and third-grade level, though harder words are listed at the end of each lesson for students with a more advanced reading vocabulary. You might use the Spell Check on page 46 as a pretest to see which of your students are in need of these sorts. Students who spell most of the words (90%) on the Spell Check correctly may go on to the study of less common long-vowel patterns, such as the ones presented in Sorts 19 to 24.

Teaching Tips

Most of these six sorts contains 19 to 21 words plus three to four column headers. Key words have been bolded on the sort sheet and these should be placed at the top of each column. Key words are the most frequently occurring words of that particular spelling pattern. Oddballs are high-frequency words whose pattern violates the dominant pattern-to-sound correspondence. For example, the word *said* is an oddball because it does not contain the long -*a* sound even though it has the CVVC pattern associated with the long -*a* sound. See Chapter 6 of *WTW* for more information about teaching high-frequency words.

33

If your students seem to be catching on to the CVVC pattern quickly, speed up your pace. A slower pace is suggested in *WTW* and additional words and sorts may be found in the *WTW* Appendix. Whatever pace your students need, be sure to provide ample opportunities to sort first by sound, and then by pattern. Ultimately you want your students to be able to categorize words by sound and pattern simultaneously. See the table on page 18 of Standard Weekly Routines for activities that will provide the practice students need to master these patterns.

Literature Connection

When possible, share books that contain a number of words with the targeted spelling feature. For example, *Frog and Toad Together* (Lobel, 1971) is a natural connection with the short- and long-vowel sounds for *o* and contains many examples of the CVCe and CVVC patterns.

SORT 13   SHORT -*A* AND LONG -*A* (CVCe AND CVVC)

Demonstrate

(See page 40.) Prepare the words to use for teacher-directed modeling. You will also need a short -*a* symbol and a long -*a* symbol from the symbol template in the back of the book to use as headers for the sound sort.

Read and discuss the meanings of any unfamiliar words. Be sure to point out the homophones *main* and *mane* and discuss their meaning. Tell your students that the other *mane*, the hair on a lion's or horse's head, is spelled with a different spelling pattern because it has a different meaning. Ask if anyone sees other homophones in the set (*tail* and *tale*) and discuss their meanings as well. Students might add a small drawing to their word cards to help them associate the meaning and spelling. Ask your students what they notice about the spelling of these words. Proceed to demonstrate a two-step sort: (1) sort by sound; then, (2) sort by pattern.

Sort by Sound

Display a short -*a* symbol, a long -*a* symbol from the Appendix, and the word *oddball* at the top of three separate columns. Do not use the pattern headers (CVC, CVCe, CVVC) yet. Tell your students that the short -*a* symbol stands for the short -*a* sound in the middle of such words as *black*. Segment the middle vowel sound so they know where to focus their attention (e.g., /bl/ /a/ /ck/). Next, explain that the long -*a* symbol stands for the long -*a* sound in the middle of words such as *space* or *rain* where you can hear the letter *a* say its name. Again, segment the middle vowel sound to make the long -*a* sound and location explicit. Finally, begin the **sound sort.** Model the placement of a key word, segment the middle vowel, and explain how to sort the rest of the words: *Here is the word* rain. *R-ai-n.* Rain *has a long* -a *sound in the middle so I will put it under the long* -a *symbol with* space. *Now who can help me sort the rest of these words?* Continue on in this vein having the students help you sort all the words by sound. Warn your students to be on the lookout for two oddballs (*said* and *want*) and see if they can spot them without your help. When all the words have been sorted, read them in columns and check for any that need to be changed: *Do all of these words sound alike in the middle? Do we need to move any?*

Note: Some of your students may have trouble with the word *camp*. The nasal sound made by the letter *m* makes it difficult to segment the medial vowel sound apart from the nasal. Tell your students to pronounce the word without the nasal (*cap*) to see if they can hear the vowel sound that way.

● Sort by Pattern

Ask your students what they notice about the words in the long -*a* column: *Could we put any of those words together?* Create two columns with *space* and *rain* as headers and work with your students to sort all the long -*a* words in a **pattern sort**. Ask them to describe what they notice about the pattern of letters in each column and then display the CVC, CVCe, and CVVC as pattern headers. Label the consonant-vowel-consonant in *black*, the consonant-vowel-consonant-silent *e* pattern (CVCe) in *space*, and the consonant-vowel-vowel-consonant pattern (CVVC) in *rain*. Ask your students why *said* and *want* are oddballs. Help them understand that even though they are spelled with the CVC and CVVC patterns they do not have the expected sounds.

Sort by Sound and Pattern

Leave up the pattern headers and key words and then mix up all the words. Repeat the sort, categorizing this time by vowel sound and by long-vowel patterns at the same time. Model how to **check** the sort by reading down each column paying particular attention to the oddballs, then **reflect** about how the words in each column are alike. The sort will end up looking like this:

CVC	CVCe		CVVC		oddball
black*	**space**	*tale*	**rain**	*tail*	said*
rash	frame	*mane*	brain	*main*	want*
flash	place		paint	chain	
camp	blame		train	faint	

● *High-frequency word; homophones are in italics.

Check, Reflect, and Extend

Give each student a copy of the sort and assign the task of cutting out the words and sorting them individually using the three headers and key words. Remind students how to check their sort by reading down each column to check for sound and pattern. On subsequent days students should repeat the sort several times. See Standard Weekly Routines (page 18) for follow-up activities to this basic sorting lesson.

This is a good time to start a homophone collection. Students can also add the homophones to a special section of their word study notebooks and illustrate the meaning with a picture and/or sentence.

Suggested Words for Word-O.   *space, frame, brain, train, camp*

Additional Words.   *slam, glad, bang, bank, gasp, lamp, smash, stamp, crash, trace, paste, crane, waste, waist* (more homophones), *bait, claim, snail, saint, braid, plaid* (oddball)

SORT 14   SHORT -*O* AND LONG -*O* (CVCe AND CVVC)

Demonstrate, Sort, Check, and Reflect

(See page 41.) In this sort the *oddball* column header has been dropped to make way for more words, but students can sort oddballs (*love* and *none*) to the side. Read and discuss the meaning of the words and be sure to note the homophones *rode* and *road*. The word *knock* is worth a second look to discuss the silent *k* at the beginning as well as its use in expressions such as "knock it off" or "don't knock it." Introduce the sort in a manner similar to Sort 13. First, sort by sound using the short -*o* and long -*o* headers from the Appendix on page 138; then, sort by pattern using the key words *rode* and *road* as headers. You could also begin the lesson with an open sort by cutting off the headers. Ask your students to cut apart their words and see if they can discover the categories for themselves before they come to the group sort under your direction. You might ask students if they can brainstorm other words that rhyme with the oddball *love* (*dove, shove, glove*) to find that there is a small collection of these words that work the same way.

CVC	CVCe	CVVC		
box	***rode***	***road***	foam	love
knock	stone	float	load	one*
stop	chose	boat	goal	
drop	slope	goat	toad	
	whole	soap	coat	

*High-frequency word; homophones are in italics.

Extend

Give each student a copy of the sort and assign the task of cutting out the words and sorting them individually in the same way they did in the group. On subsequent days, students should repeat the sorting activity several times and complete the standard weekly routines in their word study notebook. Blind sorts will be very important to help students associate the correct pattern with particular words and they will need to define the homophones for their partners to sort.

Suggested Words for Word-O. *chose, toad, boat, foam, lock*

Additional Words. *shop, trot, block, song, cove, doze, drove, whole, quote, shone, lone, oak, soak, croak, groan, moat, goal, coast, none* (oddball)

SORT 15   SHORT -*U* AND LONG -*U* (CVCe AND CVVC)

Demonstrate, Sort, Check, and Reflect

(See page 42.) The sort is somewhat different from previous sorts because the most frequent CVVC pattern for the long -*u* sound, in one syllable words, is spelled *oo*. Although the *ui* pattern is quite limited, we include it here with *Common Long-Vowel Patterns* because it is also a CVVC pattern. One of the oddballs in this sort, *build*, contains the *ui* pattern but not the long -*u* sound. *From* is a high-frequency word that has the short -*u* sound but is spelled with *o*. No oddball header is provided, however, because students should be accustomed to finding "the odd ones out" by now and putting them to the side when they sort. Key words have been bolded and should be placed at the top under each header. Read and discuss the meaning of the words, then introduce the sort in a manner similar to sorts 13 and 14. First, sort by sound; then, sort by pattern.

CVC	CVCe	CVVC	CVVC	
crust	**cube**	**food**	**fruit**	build
bump	dude	bloom	suit	from*
skunk	prune	smooth	juice	
trust		broom		
		mood		
		moon		
		spoon		
		tooth		

*High-frequency word

● Extend

Have students complete the standard weekly routines in their word study notebook: writing sorts, word operations, blind or no-peeking sorts, and so on. Students may struggle to find more words in a word hunt as there are not a lot of single-syllable long -u words with these patterns.

Suggested Words for Word-O.   *bump, dude, bloom, spoon, food*

Additional Words.   *cluck, stuff, chunk, rust, fuss, dusk, blush, gust, crude, chute, muse, mute, fume, goof, loop, scoop, loom, booth, cruise, bruise*

SORT 16   SHORT -*E* AND LONG -*E* (CVVC)

Demonstrate, Sort, Check, and Reflect

(See page 43.) Like Sort 15, this sort includes two CVVC patterns for the long -*e* sound: *ee* and *ea*. Conveniently, the homophones *week* and *weak* are included to call attention to the fact that words with different meanings must have different spellings to tell them apart when we read and spell. Read and discuss the meaning of the words, then introduce the sort in a manner similar to Sorts 13, 14, and 15. You might also cut off the headers so that your students can do this as an open sort. By now they should be good at sorting by sound and looking for patterns! *Been* is an oddball.

CVC	CVVC -ee		CVVC -ea		
next*	**seem***	sweep	**eat***	clean	been*
web	keep	teeth	heat	*weak*	
less	green	feet	team	leaf	
set	sleep	*week*	speak	teach	

*High-frequency word; homophones are in italics.

Extend

Have students complete the standard weekly routines in their word study notebook: writing sorts, word operations, word hunts, blind or no-peeking writing sorts, and so on. The Sheep Game described in Chapter 6 of *WTW* provides practice with the *ee* and *ea* patterns.

Suggested Words for Word-O.   *next, sleep, heat, weak, teach*

Additional Words.   *rent, spell, press, check, chest, stem, pest, speech, speed, greed, sleeve, fleet, sleek, deed, reef, jeep, creep, creek, least, peach, deal, meal, treat*

SORT 17   "THE DEVIL SORT" SHORT -*E* (CVC AND CVVC) AND LONG -*E* (CVVC)

Demonstrate, Sort, Check, and Reflect

(See page 44.) Sort 17 is hard because it includes two CVVC patterns for the long -*e* sound (*ee* and *ea*) and two patterns for the short -*e* sound: CVC and CVVC. It is called "The Devil Sort" because the *ea* pattern is used to spell both the short -*e* and the long -*e* sound. Fortunately, many of the short -*e ea* words rhyme, so if you point this out to your students they will be able to remember them as a group: *dead, head, lead,* and *bread* all rhyme and they all end in *ead*.

Be sure to read and discuss the meaning of the words, especially the pronunciation and meaning of the word *lead*. The word *lead* is a homograph and can be pronounced with either a short or long -*e* sound, so it may be sorted in either sound category. Discuss the shift in meaning that accompanies the shift in the vowel sound. The oddball *great* is a high-frequency word that contains the *ea* pattern but has a long -*a* sound instead of a long -*e* sound. Discussing these will enrich your students' word knowledge.

After discussing the words, introduce the sort in a manner similar to the previous four sorts or challenge your students with an open sort. Use the long -*e* and short -*e* headers from the Appendix to sort first by sound, then use the key word headers to sort by the patterns of CVC and CVVC. Remind your students that they have sorted the CVVC pattern before and it was always associated with the long-vowel sound. Now, they will learn some short -*e* words that have the same pattern.

Short -*e* CVC	Short -*e* CVVC	Long -*e* CVVC -*ee*	Long -*e* CVVC -*ea*	
when*	dead	trees	each*	great
sled	head	street	reach	
	bread	queen	seat	
	breath	sweet	dream	
	death		*lead*	
	lead		steam	
			beach	
			east	

*High-frequency word; homophones and homographs in italics.

Extend

After students have repeated this sort many times, have them complete the standard weekly routines in their word study notebook. Have them use *lead* in sentences.

Suggested Words for Word-O.   *bread, street, reach, steam, east*

Additional Words.   *swept, shelf, wealth, breast, health, tread, beef, geese, breeze, peel, greet, steel, steal, sneak, beam, flea, peak, leak, leash, steak, break* (oddballs)

SORT 18   REVIEW FOR CVVC PATTERN (*AI-OA-EE-EA*)

Demonstrate, Sort, Check, and Reflect

(See page 45.) This is a review sort for the CVVC patterns for the vowels *a, o,* and *e*. The CVVC patterns for *u* are not included in this review because the *oo* pattern for the long -*u* sound is quite memorable by virtue of the double *oo*, and the *ui* pattern has few exemplars. If you wish to include the *oo* and *ui* patterns for the long -*u* sound in this CVVC review, simply recycle the long -*u* word cards from Sort 15 and add them in. Otherwise, these 24 new words contain the familiar CVVC pattern and all but four represent the long-vowel sound. The four short vowels contain the *ea* pattern for the short -*e*. Headers are not included here because you will want your students to sort by sound and by pattern on their own after your demonstration. Alternatively, you can challenge your students to do an open sort and determine their own categories. At this point, an open sort will give you diagnostic information about how the students are thinking about pattern-to-sound consistencies.

First read and discuss these new words. The homograph *read* is worthy of discussion because the verb tense changes depending on whether you pronounce it with a short or long -*e* sound. This word may be sorted with the *ea* pattern for either the short -*e* group or the long -*e* group, depending on pronunciation. Remind students of a similar phenomenon with the word *lead* in the previous sort. Many students are likely to be unfamiliar with the word *dread*, so be sure to use this word in a meaningful sentence and talk about its meaning. Several of these words begin with the complex consonant cluster *thr*. The word *three* will be familiar to the students but take the time to point out the *thr* in *thread* and *throat*.

After your discussion, demonstrate how to sort these words by vowel sound (long -*a*, long -*e*, long -*o*, and short -*e*). Then sort the long -*e* group into two columns by pattern. Mix up the words and then model sorting by sound and pattern simultaneously. It is helpful if you "think aloud" as you sort and model your mental processes. Students can create their own headers by labeling or underlining the pattern in a key word. The sort will look something like this:

w<u>ai</u>t	thr<u>ea</u>d	n<u>ee</u>d	b<u>ea</u>st	t<u>oa</u>st
trail	*read**	sheep	leak	coast
sail	deaf	wheel	neat	moan
rail	meant	three*	pea	throat
	dread	sheets	cream	
		cheek	*read**	

*High-frequency word; homographs are in italics.

Extend

After students have repeated this sort many times, have them complete the standard weekly routines in their word study notebook. Pull out *thread, three,* and *throat.* Brainstorm additional words with the beginning blend (throw, threw, threat, thrill, throne, through) and acknowledge that the blend can be hard to spell. (Sort 38 will focus on thr.)

Suggested Words for Word-O.   *wheel, cream, pea, moan, rail*

Note: *Word Operations on these words are likely to result in the creation of other homophones whose meanings bear discussion (substitute* st *for the* wh *of* wheel *and get* steel*).*

SPELL CHECK 3   ASSESSING THE CVVC LONG-VOWEL PATTERN FOR A, E, O, AND U

(See page 46.) The spelling of long vowels following the consonant-vowel-vowel-consonant (CVVC) pattern is assessed with the Spell Check for CVVC Patterns. All of the words pictured have been presented previously in Sorts 13 to 18. Name each picture, and then ask your students to write the spelling of the word on the lines provided. Students can also complete this independently. Following are the words assessed.

1. leaf	**2.** suit	**3.** beach	**4.** rain
5. toast	**6.** teeth	**7.** chain	**8.** peach
9. road	**10.** feet	**11.** mail	**12.** queen
13. pea	**14.** toad	**15.** fruit	**16.** broom
17. sail	**18.** soap	**19.** spoon	**20.** coat

SORT 13 Short -a and Long -a (CVCe and CVVC)

ă CVC	ā CVCe	ā CVVC
oddball	**space**	**rain**
black	mane	tale
brain	paint	place
rash	blame	train
main	faint	want
chain	camp	tail
said	frame	flash

SORT 14   Short -o and Long -o (CVCe and CVVC)

ŏ CVC	ō CVCe	ō CVVC
box	**rode**	**road**
chose	boat	love
goat	soap	knock
slope	foam	load
whole	one	goal
stop	toad	coat
float	drop	stone

SORT 15   Short -u and Long -u (CVCe and CVVC)

ŭ CVC	ū CVCe	ūi CVVC
o͞o CVVC	cube	food
fruit	crust	bloom
smooth	suit	from
dude	skunk	broom
mood	bump	juice
trust	build	moon
prune	spoon	tooth

SORT 16 Short -*e* and Long -*e* (CVVC)

ĕ CVC	ēe CVVC	ēa CVVC
next	**seem**	**eat**
green	team	been
sleep	web	speak
clean	keep	sweep
teeth	heat	week
weak	less	set
leaf	teach	feet

SORT 17   "The Devil Sort" Short -e (CVC and CVVC) and Long -e (CVVC)

ĕ CVC	ēa CVVC	ēe CVVC
ēa CVVC	when	dead
trees	each	reach
head	queen	east
street	bread	seat
dream	great	lead
steam	sled	sweet
breath	beach	death

SORT 18   Review for CVVC Pattern (*ai, oa, ee, ea*)

wait	read	need
beast	toast	wheel
sheep	leak	coast
trail	deaf	three
neat	moan	sheets
meant	rail	cheek
pea	throat	dread
cream	sail	thread

Spell Check 3   Assessing the CVVC Long-Vowel Pattern for *a, e, o,* and *u*

Name _____

1. _____	2. _____
3. _____	4. _____
5. _____	6. _____
7. _____	8. _____
9. _____	10. _____
11. _____	12. _____
13. _____	14. _____
15. _____	16. _____
17. _____	18. _____
19. _____	20. _____

Unit IV   Less Common Long-Vowel Patterns

NOTES FOR THE TEACHER

Background and Objectives

This unit presents a variety of other long-vowel patterns for *a, o, u,* and *i.* The long-vowel patterns introduced in these sorts are less common because they occur in fewer single-syllable words. In this unit the open syllable is introduced in words such as *lay, chew,* and *cry.* An open syllable ends in a vowel sound as opposed to being "closed" with a consonant that you can hear and is represented as CV or CVV. Other less common long-vowel patterns introduced in this section include the CVCC patterns in words such as *told, mild,* or *light.* We have increased the cognitive load in these sorts by including more words and less familiar words as well as some new patterns. Although the open syllable and the CVCC patterns are the new spelling features introduced in this section, previously studied vowel sounds and patterns (CVC, CVCe, and CVVC) reappear in new words and provide review as well as a starting point for comparison. Students will:

- Review the short-vowel sound and spellings and the CVCe spelling for long vowels
- Learn spelling patterns for long -*a* (*ai* and *ay*), long -*o* (*oa* and *ow*), long -*u* (*ew* and *ue*), and long -*i* (*igh* and *y*)
- Learn the VCC pattern for long -*i* and long -*o*

Targeted Learners

Sorts 19 to 24 are designed for middle within word pattern stage spellers who correctly spell the CVCe and CVVC patterns but are using but confusing the less common long-vowel patterns. They might spell the word *told,* TOALD; or the word *mild,* MILED. Most of the words in these sorts are on a third- to fourth-grade level. Where possible, more words are listed at the end of each lesson and they are usually harder words. You might use the Spell Check on page 61 as a pretest to see which of your students are in need of these sorts. Students who spell most of the words on the Spell Check correctly (90%) may move on to the study of *r*-influenced vowels or diphthongs introduced in Sorts 25 to 35.

Teaching Tips

Each of these six sorts contains 23 to 24 words plus four column headers. Key words have been bolded and these should be placed at the top of each column. As always, key words are the most frequently occurring words of that particular spelling pattern. Oddballs are either high-frequency words whose patterns violate the dominant pattern-to-sound correspondence or are words that encompass features of two or more categories. Although Sorts 19 to 24 are decidedly more difficult than the previous 18 sorts, the recursive nature of word study makes it possible to generalize the new patterns introduced here across the vowels. This is the objective of Sort 24 that reviews the CVCC, CVVC, and open syllable across all four vowels.

By this time your students should be adept at sorting by sound and by pattern. Because the focus of these sorts is on less common vowel patterns, and only a few short-vowel words are included in each sort, you might be able to speed up the introductory process of sorting by sound first before sorting by pattern and try sorting by sound and pattern simultaneously. If students are experienced sorters, you may come to rely more on open sorts in which they are asked to cut apart their words and sort them into categories of sound and pattern before they come to the group lesson. Asking capable students to do these open sorts while you are working directly with another group can make managing several groups easier. Open sorts are also diagnostic and allow you to see what students are noticing about the orthography. You may want to cut off the headers before duplicating the words for open sorts. Also, remember to enlarge the sorts when copying to increase the size.

Standard Weekly Routines can be found on page 18. This is a good time to introduce students to speed sorts if you have not done so already. Students in the middle to upper elementary grades respond well to the challenge of timing themselves and then practicing in order to improve their times.

Literature Connection

When possible, share books and poems that contain some words that are spelled with the targeted feature. For example, *Stellaluna* (Cannon, 1993) contains many examples of the VCC and open-syllable long-vowel patterns.

SORT 19   SHORT -*A* AND LONG -*A* (CVCe, CVVC -*AI*, AND OPEN SYLLABLE -*AY*)

Demonstrate

(See page 55.) Prepare set of words to use for modeling. Begin as usual by reading and discussing the meaning of the words. Then, ask students what they notice about the spelling of the words. In this case they all have the letter *a*. Next, display the pattern labels to head each of the four columns as well as the bolded key word. Tell your students that they will learn a new pattern for the long -*a* sound in this sort: the *ay* pattern. However, if your students have had experience sorting, this should be a fairly easy open sort for them to do on their own before the group discussion.

Compare each of the key words to the pattern label to be sure that students are clear about what the *C*s and *V*s represent. Model how to sort several words and then begin to involve your students in sorting the rest of the words. *They* is an oddball in this sort and will be easily recognized as having the sound but not the pattern. The word *raise* merits some discussion because it has the CVVC pattern *ai* in addition to an *e* at the end. Explain that the *e* at the end of *raise* is not the same kind of silent *e* that makes the medial vowel "say its name" as in the CVCe pattern they have previously sorted. The word *raise* may or may not be considered an oddball. (Sort 40 explores *ce, ve, se,* and *ze* endings.)

Sort, Check, and Reflect

After you demonstrate several words (or the entire sort if you think students need that much support), the students should sort their own words under the headers and then read down each column to check for sound and pattern.

Help your students reflect on this sort. See if they notice that all of the *ay* words end in a long-vowel sound. Tell your students that a syllable or a one-syllable word that ends in a long-vowel sound is called an *open syllable*. One way of labeling an open-syllable pattern is to label it a CV or CVV pattern, since the *y* acts as a vowel in these long *-a* words. (Note: When one-syllable words end with the long *-a* sound they will generally be spelled with *ay*. *Sleigh, weigh,* and *neigh* are exceptions but then they are homophones of *slay, way,* and *nay*.)

CVC	CVCe	CVVC -*ai*	CVV -*ay*	oddball
glass	**trade**	**nail**	**day***	they*
stand	brave	grain	stay	
past	slave	aid	play*	
	shape	raise	clay	
	taste	gain	tray	
			may*	
			gray	
			pray	
			say*	

*High-frequency word

Extend

Have your students **extend** this sort by completing the recommended standard weekly routines for Sorts 19 to 24: repeated word sorts, writing sorts, speed sorts, word hunts, and blind or no-peeking sorts. A homework form can be found in the Appendix.

Additional Words.   *grand, brass, task, tramp, grave, graze, lame, rate, slate, stale, faith, stain, fail, praise, Spain, lay, jay, sway, ray, slay, sleigh, weigh, neigh* (oddballs)

SORT 20   SHORT -*O* AND LONG -*O* (CVCe, CVVC -*OA*, AND OPEN SYLLABLE -*OW*)

(See page 56.) Introduce the sort in a manner similar to Sort 19 or you might want to try an open sort in which the students sort on their own before any discussion. As you read and discuss the words, point out the word *know* and compare it to the homophone *no*. Discuss the silent *k* at the beginning. Remind them of the word *knock* from Sort 14. See if they can spot another word that has a silent letter at the beginning (*wrote*). Tell your students that they will learn a new pattern for the long *-o* sound.

Demonstrate, Sort, Check, and Reflect

Demonstrate this sort as in previous sorts. The oddball *whose* will require some discussion because it has the CVCe pattern but does not contain the long *-o* sound.

CVC	CVCe	CVVC -oa	CVV -ow	
long*	**froze**	**coal**	**show**	whose
stock	globe	coach	blow	
	wrote	roast	slow	
	close	oat	grow	
		loaf	flow	
		roam	throw	
			row	
			snow	
			mow	
			know	

*High-frequency word

Help your students **reflect** on this sort. See what they think about the *ow* pattern in relation to the open-syllable discussion in the previous sort. Remind them that when a syllable or a one-syllable word ends with a long-vowel sound, it is called an *open syllable*. One way of labeling the open-syllable pattern is by labeling it in a CV or CVV pattern since *w* acts like a vowel, not a consonant. Brainstorm some other long -*o* open-syllable words with the CV pattern: *no, go, so, ho, yoyo,* and the CVV pattern: *toe, hoe, doe, foe,* and *woe.*

Extend

Have your students **extend** this sort by completing the recommended standard weekly routines. The Word Study Uno game described in Chapter 6 of *WTW* is set up to review long -*o* patterns. You might dictate the sentence: *Show the coach how you throw a slow ball close to home plate.*

Additional Words.   *dock, prompt, stomp, blond, sole, dome, pose, quote, rove, yoke, Rome, lope, zone, cloak, loaves, boast, coax, loan, own, bow, crow, glow, tow, flown, broad* (oddball)

SORT 21   SHORT -*U* AND LONG -*U* (OPEN SYLLABLE -*EW* AND -*UE*)

(See page 57.) This sort is full of homophones. If you do this as an open sort you can save the discussion of the homophones and their meaning for after the sort. Remind students that when words sound the same but have a different meaning, the words have a different spelling pattern so we can tell them apart. Talk about the silent *k* in the word *knew* and how *knew* is past tense for *know,* a word they had in the long -*o* sort. Remind them that when a syllable or a word that is one syllable ends with a long-vowel sound, it is called an *open syllable*. One way of labeling the open-syllable pattern is by labeling in a CV or CVV pattern, since *w* acts like a vowel.

Demonstrate, Sort, Check, and Reflect

Demonstrate this sort as in the previous two sorts. There are three oddballs in this sort: *truth, do,* and *sew.* You will need to give your students a heads-up about the pronunciation of *sew.* After finding the oddballs in this sort, discuss their spelling pattern in terms of the vowel sound normally associated with that pattern, and then clarify the vowel sound they actually have. Discuss the new patterns for the long -*u* sound. Ask if anyone can tell which two spelling patterns alternate in *blue* and *blew.* Explain that the final *w* in the *ew* pattern acts like a vowel so that *dew, blew, flew,* and so on end in a vowel sound, just like the long -*o* words that ended in *ow* did.

CVC	CVV -ew	CVV -ue	
thumb	*new* *	*blue*	truth
plump	grew	*flue*	*do* *
brush	chew	*due*	*sew*
stuck	few	glue	
junk	*flew*	true	
trunk	*knew*		
	stew		
	blew		
	dew		
	crew		

*High-frequency word; homophones are in italics.

Extend

Extend this sort by completing the recommended standard weekly routines. You might dictate the sentence: *I knew he did not have a clue about the homework that was due in a few hours.*

Additional Words. crumb, tusk, husk, slump, snuff, shrewd, strewn, whew, screw, brew, hue, clue, sue, cue, cruel, fuel. (Words spelled with *oo* could also be contrasted with the words in this sort but we have included them in Sorts 15 and 32.)

SORT 22 SHORT -*I* AND LONG -*I* (CVCe, CVCC -*IGH*, AND CV OPEN SYLLABLE -*Y*)

(See page 58.) Begin as usual by reading and discussing the meaning of the words, especially the homophones *write* and *right*. Next, display the short -*i* and long -*i* symbols with the pattern labels to head each of the four columns. Review the CVC pattern associated with the short -*i* sound and the CVCe pattern for the long -*i* sound. (If necessary, revisit Sort 8.) Tell your students they will learn two new patterns for the long -*i* sound in this sort.

Demonstrate, Sort, Check, and Reflect

Demonstrate the sort as in previous sorts, but with so few short-vowel words, skip the sound sort. *Live* is a homograph that can be pronounced two ways with two different meanings. It might be sorted as an oddball.

CVC	CVCe	CVCC -*igh*	CV -*y*	
quick	**white** *	**might**	**why** *	*live*
quit	twice	high	cry	
	quite	night	sky	
	fine	bright	fly	
	write	fight	try	
		flight	shy	
		sight		
		sigh		
		right		

*High-frequency word; homophones or homographs are in italics.

Discuss how the *gh* of the *igh* pattern is silent but the *gh* signals that the *i* sound is long. Explain that we can label the *igh* pattern CVCC, because the vowel *i* is followed by two consonants: the *g* and the *h*. Remind students that the open-syllable pattern in words like *why*, *cry*, and *sky* can be labeled CV, because the *y* acts as a vowel in these long -*i* words. The open long -*i* sound can also be spelled with -*ie* (*pie, tie, lie, die*) and -*ye* (*dye, lye, rye*).

Extend

Extend this sort by completing the recommended standard weekly routines. The Race-track game described and illustrated in Chapter 6 of *WTW* shows how it can be adapted for a review of long -*i* patterns. You might dictate the sentence: *Last night I had quite a fright when I saw live white mice!* Pull out *quick*, *quit*, and *quite* and review the initial sound of qu. Ask what sound the u represents in these words (/w/) and discuss how it is not part of the vowel pattern as it is in *suit*.

Additional Words.   *filth, risk, swift, twist, crime, prime, chime, lime, spice, lice, mite, rise, fright, slight, thigh, spry, dry, sly, rye, lye, dye*

SORT 23   SHORT -*I* AND LONG -*I* (VCC) WITH SHORT -*O* AND LONG -*O* (VCC)

(See page 59.) This sort focuses on two additional VCC patterns for both the long -*i* and long -*o* sounds. These are contrasted with short -*i* and a sound for *o* that is short in some dialects but not in others. Listen carefully to how you and your students say the sounds in *lost*, *moth*, *soft*, and *cost*. The sound may be slightly different from the short -*o* sound in *cot* but chances are they are all pronounced with the same sound and can be put together by sound. They are included here because of the similarity in patterns (*lost-most*, *moth-both*). *Wind* is a homograph whose different pronunciations and meanings should be discussed.

Demonstrate, Sort, Check, and Reflect

Because the patterns overlap in this sort, it is best to sort first by sound, and then sort by patterns within each sound category.

VCC -*i*	VCC -*i*	VCC -*o*	VCC -*o*	oddball
film	**find***	**lost**	**most***	friend*
fist	wild	moth	told	
wind	child	soft	cold	
	kind*	cost	both*	
	mind		roll	
	blind		scold	
	wind		gold	
			post	
			ghost	

*High-frequency word; homographs are in italics.

Additional Words.   *mild, mint, hint, sift, tilt, hind, jolt, colt, bold, host, mold, volt, bolt, loss, moss, broth, comb*

● SORT 24   REVIEW OF LONG-VOWEL PATTERNS

(See page 60.) This sort reviews the four long-vowel patterns that apply to all five long-vowel sounds for *a, e, i, o,* and *u.* The headers represent the patterns to be reviewed: CVCC, CVVC, CVCe, and open-syllable patterns CV and CVV. There are 23 new words following these four familiar long-vowel patterns. After going over the word meanings, the words should be sorted first by their long-vowel sound. Use headers from the Appendix or create your own. Reflect with your students on the variety of ways in which each of the long-vowel sounds can be spelled.

Long -*a*	Long -*e*	Long -*i*	Long -*o*	Long -*u*
wave	bleed	grind	sold	clue
jail	steep	slide	glow	school*
way*	sneak	dry	hold	drew
	scene	bind	tone	pool
	feast	light	crow	
			soak	

*High-frequency word

Next introduce the four pattern headers and challenge the students to resort all the words under one of them. The final sort will look like this:

CVCC	CVVC	CVCe	CV & CVV
sold	bleed	wave	glow
hold	steep	tone	clue
grind	sneak	slide	dry
bind	school	scene	crow
light	jail		drew
	soak		way
	pool		
	feast		

Extend

During a blind sort or no-peeking sort partners will need to decide if the sort will be by sound or pattern. Pattern will be more difficult but also more valuable.

Grand Sort.   Because this rounds up the study of long vowels you may want to challenge your students to create a grand sort that includes all the words from this unit (Sorts 19 to 23) as well as the previous unit (Sorts 13 to 18). Such a sort will reinforce the idea that patterns underlie all the short- and long-vowel sounds in English and, although oddballs exist, regularity persists overall. To prepare for the grand sort, make just one copy of each sort (13 to 23) and have students cut them apart and combine them all (omitting the headers). Then, working as a group, students should decide how to sort the words. Words can be sorted first by sound (the five long and short sounds) and then by sound and pattern. For example, under CVVC there will be long -*e* words with *ea* and with *ee* grouped together. Oddballs should constitute their own category. Ultimately students will see that most words can be sorted under one of the four pattern headers (plus CVC) in Sort 24. Such a grand sort can serve as a celebration of all that students have learned so far in the within word pattern stage. The words can be glued onto poster boards for display.

SPELL CHECK 4   ASSESSMENT FOR LESS COMMON LONG-VOWEL PATTERNS

This assessment can be administered as a writing sort using the form on page 61 or you can simply call the words out to be listed in a traditional way. (If you use this as a pretest it is best to do it as a single list.) All of the words assessed have been presented previously in Sorts 19 to 24. Say each word clearly, then ask your students to write it on lines provided under the correct pattern header. If you plan to grade this assessment, give 1 point for the proper placement of the word if it is written into the right category, and another point for the correct spelling of the word. Students who score at least 90% on a pretest can move on to other features. Following are the 20 words being assessed.

1. gold	**2.** brave	**3.** try	**4.** kind
5. grain	**6.** stay	**7.** child	**8.** slide
9. grow	**10.** light	**11.** coach	**12.** few
13. rule	**14.** sneak	**15.** true	**16.** quite
17. pool	**18.** close	**19.** bleed	**20.** clue

SORT 19   Short -*a* and Long -*a* (CVCe, CVVC -*ai*, and Open Syllable -*ay*)

ă CVC	ā CVCe	āi CVVC
āy CVV	**day**	**trade**
nail	**glass**	stay
raise	grain	brave
play	clay	stand
slave	they	tray
may	gray	gain
taste	aid	say
shape	past	pray

SORT 20   Short -o and Long -o (CVCe, CVVC -oa, and Open Syllable -ow)

ŏ CVC	ō CVCe	ōa CVVC
ōw CVV	**froze**	**coal**
show	**long**	slow
globe	coach	blow
grow	whose	snow
roast	flow	throw
row	stock	close
oat	mow	know
wrote	roam	loaf

SORT 21   Short -*u* and Long -*u* (Open Syllable -*ew* and -*ue*)

ŭ CVC	e̅w̅ CVV	u̅e CVV
thumb	**new**	**blue**
grew	truth	flue
plump	chew	do
due	brush	glue
few	junk	true
stuck	flew	stew
knew	crew	blew
dew	trunk	sew

SORT 22   Short -*i* and Long -*i* (*CVCe*, *CVCC* -*igh*, and *CV* Open Syllable -*y*)

ĭ CVC	ī CVCe	īgh VCC
y = ī CV	**might**	**quick**
why	**white**	high
night	twice	quite
cry	bright	sky
quit	fight	fly
flight	sight	fine
try	live	write
sigh	shy	right

SORT 23   Short -*i* and Long -*i* (VCC) with Short -*o* and Long -*o* (VCC)

ĭ VCC	ī VCC	ŏ VCC
ō VCC	**find**	**most**
film	**lost**	child
moth	cost	both
kind	roll	fist
cold	scold	gold
told	wild	soft
post	friend	wind
blind	ghost	mind

SORT 24   Review of Long-Vowel Patterns

CVCC	CVVC	CVCe
CV & CVV **Open syllable**	sold	bleed
wave	glow	hold
steep	tone	clue
grind	sneak	slide
dry	crow	bind
school	jail	soak
scene	drew	light
pool	way	feast

● Spell Check 4   Assessment for Less Common Long-Vowel Patterns

Name _____

1. **CVCC**	2. **CVCe**
_____	_____
_____	_____
_____	_____
_____	_____
_____	_____
_____	_____

3. **CVVC**	4. **CV or CVV Open Syllable**
_____	_____
_____	_____
_____	_____
_____	_____
_____	_____

Unit V R-Influenced Vowel Patterns

NOTES FOR THE TEACHER

Background and Objectives

This unit presents the spelling patterns for *r*-influenced (or *r*-controlled) vowels for *a, e, i, o,* and *u*. This is a difficult feature with overlapping sounds and patterns (*ear* is used to spell several sounds as in *gear, earn, bear,* and *heart*) Homophones and oddballs are plentiful. Why is this the case? Probably because the /r/ sound is linguistically known as a liquid (*l* is the other liquid) and it has vowel-like qualities. It often "robs" the vowel it follows of its own sound and leaves behind a new sound like the /ar/ in *car* or the /ur/ sound in *her, sir,* and *fur*. Although we can isolate the vowel in a word like *jam* as /j/a/m/ we really cannot separate the vowel in *car* or *her* from the consonant that follows. *R*-influenced vowels seem to be susceptible to change over time so that the pronunciation of words has shifted while the spelling has remained the same. In addition, *r*s are sometimes dropped in certain dialects at the end of words (as in "pahk" for *park*) and then inserted in others ("idear" for *idea*). *R* is a trilled sound in Spanish and it does not even exist in some languages, especially in the final position after a vowel. This means that English Language Learners will have difficulty attending to and producing the different *r*-influenced sounds.

Not surprisingly, many students are stymied by *r*-influenced vowels and end up spelling simple words like *skirt*, SKURT; or even *girl* as GRIL. Fortunately, most *r*-influenced spelling patterns follow the same long-vowel patterns already studied, so this sequence of sorts will capitalize on this happy state of affairs by comparing and contrasting the short- and long-vowel patterns for the *r*-influenced words. There are many homophones among the *r*-influenced words but you will find that the use of meaning will help focus your students' attention on the vowel patterns that distinguish them. *Stair* and *stare, fair* and *fare, pair* and *pare* are all distinguishable by the long-vowel patterns learned in the earlier sorts in this supplement. Meaning will help straighten out even the most difficult of the *r*-influenced words, the schwa + r sound /ər/. The *schwa* is a vowel in an unstressed syllable such as the /uh/ sound in the first syllable of *about*, or a vowel in a single-syllable word that has been robbed of its own identity by the stronger sounds that surround it. Such is the case with words like *fir* and *fur, heard* and *herd, per* and *purr*. In all of these little words, the *r* robs the vowel of its own identity, making it impossible to tell what vowel is in the middle by the use of sound alone. All of them sound the same, /ur/ or/ər/. Students will:

- Distinguish the *r*-influenced /a/ sounds in *car* and *air* (sometimes referred to as short and long) and learn the spellings for those sounds (*ar, air, are*)
- Distinguish the *r*-influenced /e/ sounds in *her* and *hear* (sometimes referred to as short and long) and learn the spellings for those sounds (*er, ear, eer*)

- Distinguish the *r*-influenced /i/ sounds in *bird* and *fire* (sometimes referred to as short and long) and learn the spellings for those sounds (*ir, ire, ier*)
- Learn the spellings associated with the *r*-influenced /o/ sound (*or, ore, oar*)
- Learn the spellings associated with the *r*-influenced /u/ sound (*ur, ure*)
- Learn about the influence of *w* on the sound of the vowel when it precedes *or* and *ar*.

Targeted Learners

Sorts 25 to 30 are designed for middle to late within word pattern stage spellers. Many of the words in these sorts are on a third- to fourth-grade level. You might use the Spell Check on page 77 as a pretest to see which of your students are in need of these sorts. Students who spell most of the words on the Spell Check correctly (90%) may move on to the study of the more difficult features introduced in Sorts 31 to 50.

Teaching Tips

Each of these six sorts contains from 21 to 27 words plus column headers. Key words have been bolded and these should be placed at the top of each column. As always, key words are the most frequently occurring words of that particular spelling pattern. The oddballs are words whose patterns violate the dominant pattern-to-sound correspondence. For example, the word *heard* is an oddball because it does not contain the long -*e* sound of other *ear* words like *hear* or *clear*. Many oddballs are homophones—they have a different pattern because they have a different meaning. In this unit several additional sorts are suggested to explore the feature in more depth. They can be treated as an extension to the existing sorts, something students may simply add to their word study notebooks, or you may wish to create a sort using the template in the Appendix and sort the words using the weekly routines.

  We recommend that you demonstrate the categorization of *r*-influenced spelling by first sorting by sound, and then sorting by patterns within each category of sound. Although teacher-directed sorts are described here, you may also choose to do open sorts as a first step. Remove the headers before giving students a copy of the words and ask them to discover categories on their own before sorting as a group. Remember to enlarge the sorts before duplicating to reduce waste and cutting time.

  Refer to page 18 for standard weekly routines to use with these sorts. Because so many *r*-influenced patterns are homophones, this is an ideal time to reintroduce the idea of illustrating the meaning of these homophones with carefully done drawings and thoughtful sentences. Ask your students to pick 5 to 10 words from their weekly sort and draw a picture or create a sentence that will make their meaning clear. You will need to lay down some guidelines regarding the size and expectations for detail in these drawings. Also, you will need to model how to turn simple sentences into more elaborate ones whose context shows meaning of the word. For example, use an overhead to show students how they can turn the simple sentence, *I saw a hare,* into a more elaborate version

---

Literature Connection

When possible, share books that contain a number of words with the targeted spelling feature. For example, *Wagon Wheels* (by Barbara Brennen) contains *r*-influenced words like *dirt, burn, third,* and *corn*. The *Story of Ferdinand* (by Munro Leaf) contains *cork* and *snort*, and *The Great White Man-Eating Shark* (by Margaret Mahy) has words with *ar* and *or* spellings.

such as, *I saw a brown hare hopping through the forest,* by asking such questions as, *What kind of hare?* or *Where did you see it?*

Games continue to be a good way to extend the practice of spelling features and to offer review over time. Keep games available for students to play from previous spelling features even as you introduce new ones. Familiar game formats such as Racetrack and Rummy can be adapted for *r*-influenced features. The Letter Spin game shown in Chapter 6 of *WTW* is set up to review *r*-influenced spelling patterns, and the game Treasure from the *WTW* CD-ROM is highly recommended.

SORT 25   *AR, ARE, AIR*

Demonstrate

(See page 71.) Read and discuss the words before sorting, paying particular attention to the homophones (see words in italics below). When you discuss the words again after the sorting, you and your students will probably conclude that all of these words are influenced by the sound of the /r/ but that they still work the same way as most short- and long-vowel patterns do.

First, sort the words into two columns by *sound:* short *-r* words that sound like *are* in the middle, and long *-r* words that sound like the word *air* in the middle. All of the words will fit into one of these two categories. Next, discuss the spelling patterns of most of the short *-r* words. All but one are spelled with *ar* in the middle, just as it sounds. The exception, *heart,* could be considered an oddball because it sounds like a short *-r* word but is not spelled with *ar.* Tell students that there is a homophone partner for the word *heart* spelled with an *ar*—*hart*—an old-fashioned word for a male deer. The word *heart* has a different spelling pattern since the *ar* was already taken.

Next, discuss the spelling patterns in the long *-r* group and pull out *care* and *hair* as key words. Display the *are* and *air* pattern headers and sort the long *-r* group by these patterns. The ones that do not fit may be considered oddballs. Ask if they notice any recurring spelling pattern among the oddballs. *Bear, wear,* and *pear* are all spelled with an *ear* pattern but have a long *-a,* not a long *-e,* sound. The pattern in the word *where* is unique but necessary because *ware* and *wear* are already taken. Sort 25 should look something like this:

ar		are		air		oddball	
part	dark	**care**	bare	**hair**	stair	pear	heart
start	shark	pare	fare	fair		wear	
harm		stare	hare	pair		bear	
sharp		square		chair		where*	

*High-frequency word; homophones are in italics.

Sort, Check, Reflect, and Extend

Have your students sort their own word cards under the pattern headers and key words, then check their sorts by reading down each column to check for consistency in sound and pattern. They should then record their sort in their word study notebooks declaring what they have learned in a written reflection. **Extend** this sort with write and draw activities and other standard weekly routines. Do not forget about the game Treasure from the *WTW* CD-ROM.

Additional Words.   *hart, harp, barb, scar, dark, lark, arch, glare, ware, flare, rare, snare, spare, blare, flair, lair, there, their* (oddballs)

SORT 26   ER, EAR, EER

Demonstrate

(See page 72.) Discuss the meanings of the words and ask students to look for homophones. Be sure to highlight the meaning of the word *heard* as distinct from its homophone partner *herd,* and point out the *ear* and *hear* inside of *heard* as a spelling-meaning connection. The *ear* in *hear* can also help students distinguish the homophones *here* and *hear.* You might discuss the change in verb tense between *hear* and *heard* and use them both in meaningful sentences. Sort by the patterns and then check the columns carefully for sound. Students should notice that *earth, heard,* and *learn* all contain the *ear* pattern but do not have the long *-e* sound associated with that pattern in words like *hear.* These three words should be moved to their own category.

er	ear	eer	ear = ur	oddball
her *	**hear**	**deer**	**heard**	there *
perch	fear	steer	earth	*here* *
herd	spear	cheer	learn	
fern	clear	peer		
germ	near			
clerk	*dear*			
term	year			

*High-frequency word; homophones are in italics.

Sort, Check, Reflect, and Extend

A special extension might be helpful after doing Sorts 25 and 26. Beacause the *ear* pattern is particularly challenging, students should look for all the words in both sorts with the *ear* pattern and sort them by sound as follows:

pear	hear	earth	heart
wear	fear	heard	
bear	spear	learn	
	clear		
	near		
	dear		
	year		

You might want to create another sort for more practice, exploring *ear* by using the template in the Appendix and adding or substituting additional words from the list below.

Additional Words.   *ear, beard, sear, rear, herb, perk, stern, jerk, serve, nerve, queer, sneer, leer, earn, yearn, swear, hearth*

SORT 27 IR, IRE, IER

Demonstrate

(See page 73.) Introduce the sort in a manner similar to the previous two sorts. The meaning and spelling of the oddball *fur* should be discussed and contrasted with its homophone partner *fir*, and *their* should be contrasted with the oddball from the last sort, *there*. You may prefer to categorize the words *drier, pliers, flier,* and *crier* as oddballs, too, as these words are derived from another form of the word. These *ier* words should be discussed in terms of the meaning of their base forms and the spelling changes that occur when changing the verb (*dry, fly, ply, cry*) to a noun (*drier, pliers, flier, crier*). Be sure to use these words in meaningful sentences. Most students will be unfamiliar with the meaning of the verb *ply* and may not know what *pliers* are, so you might want to bring in your toolbox! The word *higher* is not included in this but is a homophone partner to *hire*. The words *whirl, twirl,* and *swirl* are difficult words because of the presence of the /w/ sound at the beginning and because of the *l* in addition to the *r* at the end. Interestingly, these words all have similar meanings that will require discussion and maybe even physical demonstration. Happy twirling!

ir		ire	ier	oddball
girl*	*fir*	**fire**	**drier**	*fur*
first	whirl	wire	pliers	*their**
dirt	swirl	tire	flier	
third	thirst	hire	crier	
bird	chirp			
birth	skirt			
shirt	twirl			

*High-frequency word; homophones are in italics.

Sort, Check, Reflect, and Extend

Have your students sort their own word cards and check their sorts by reading down each column to check for consistency in sound and pattern. Have them record their sort in their word study notebooks and declare what they have learned in a written reflection. **Extend** this sort with write and draw activities and other standard weekly routines.

Because *r*-blends like the *fr, gr,* or *br* in easy words like *frog, grab,* and *brick* are common, some students may persist spelling *first* as FRIST, *girl* as GRIL, *bird* as BRID. If this problem persists, you might extend this sort by comparing common *r*-blends to these short -*r* words (*grill-girl, bride-bird, drip-dirt, fry-first, stir-stripe*).

Additional Words.   *firm, stir, sir, whirr, sire, spire, mire, higher, liar, friar, frier*

SORT 28 OR, ORE, OAR, W + OR

Demonstrate, Sort, Check, Reflect, and Extend

(See page 74.) R-influenced *o* words do not have the short and long distinction in sound that the r-influenced patterns for *a, e,* and *i* do. The vowel sounds in *fork, store,* and *roar* are all the same. *R*-influenced *o* words have the further distinction of having a *schwa plus r*/ər/ sound that occurs in words that start with *w*—words like *word, work,* or *worm.* In *w* plus *or* words the vowel sound is robbed of its identity because of the stronger sounds of the *w* and *r* on either side.

Introduce this sort by the patterns *or, ore, oar,* and *w* + *or.* Be sure to discuss how the sound of *or* changes after *w.* The oddballs in this sort also have the /or/ sound but have different patterns—as in *four, floor,* and *poor.* There are also six homophones in this sort, but only one homophone pair (*sore* and *soar*). In most cases, the homophone partner is a more difficult word: *board-bored, poor-pour, oar-ore* (also *or*), *four-fore* (but also *for*). The partners are included in the list of additional words below.

or	*ore*	*oar*	*w* + *or*	oddball
form	**more***	**board**	**work***	four*
fork	store	roar	word	floor
horn	shore	oar	world	door
north	tore	*soar*	worm	
corn	wore			
storm	*sore*			

*High-frequency word; homophones are in italics.

Additional Words.   *chord, ford, fort, snort, pork, sworn, for, fore, scorn, swore, forge, gorge, or, ore, coarse, bored, worse, pour, fourth, court, poor, our* (oddball)

SORT 29   UR, URE, UR-E

(See page 75.) This *r*-influenced *u* sort has only 19 words because there are simply not a lot of one-syllable words with these patterns. The words themselves are less familiar so you must be careful to bring them to life through enriched discussion and by providing robust examples. Many students may not have heard of the words *lure, churn,* or *surf.* In addition, there is considerable variation in the pronunciation of some of the *ure* words like *pure* and *cure.* Some may pronounce these words as two syllables as in *pee-your* for *pure.* You may find some students placing *pure* and *cure* in the oddball column while others may put them with the other *ure* words like *sure* and *lure.* Either way is fine. You will need to discuss the final *e* in the words *curve, nurse, purse,* and *curse,* and distinguish the *ur-e* pattern from the CVCe long-vowel pattern. You could keep these words in their own *ur-e* category because of their unique spelling pattern, or you could put them with the *ur* group because they share the same /ər/ sound in the middle. To work out these issues, we recommend introducing this sort in a two-category **sound sort** first.

Demonstrate the **sound sort,** which may look like this:

turn					*sure*
burn	hurl	surf	nurse	urge	lure
hurt	burst	purr	purse		pure
curl	churn	were	curse		cure
church	curb	curve	blurt		

Follow this with a **pattern sort** which will look like this:

ur		*ure*	*ur-e*	oddball
turn	burst	**sure***	**curve**	were*
burn	churn	lure	nurse	
hurt	surf	pure	purse	
curl	purr	cure	curse	
church	curb		urge	
hurl	blurt			

Additional Words.   *blurt, lurch, spurt, burr, purge*

SORT 30   REVIEW OF *AR*, SCHWA-PLUS-*R*, AND *OR*

Demonstrate, Sort, Check, and Reflect

(See page 76.) This last sort reviews some of the sounds and patterns covered in earlier sorts. All three homophone pairs (horse/hoarse, worn/warn, bore/boar) require discussion to establish their meanings. Sort the words by sound into three categories: *ar, schwa + r,* and *or.* Discuss with the students how words with *ar* are spelled quite regularly while words with the other two sounds are spelled in a variety of ways.

ar		*schwa + r*		*or*	
jar		earn	sir	thorn	*boar*
hard		search	lurk	*worn*	*bore*
yarn		pearl		*hoarse*	score
march		worth		*horse*	snore
		worst		core	warm
		spur		chore	*warn*

Homophones are in italics.

Extend

An interesting extension to this sort is to pull out all the words that begin with *w* from Sorts 27 and 28. Students can also be given these additional words: *worth, worse, swore, wear, swear, warm, dwarf, wart, swarm,* and *warp.* Students should be challenged to sort them and see what kind of conclusions they can draw about these words. Students will find that the *w* seems to exert a special control on words as shown in the sort below. You might create this as an additional sort using the template in the Appendix.

w + or = ur	*w + or = or*	*w + ar = or*	*w + ear = air*
work	*wore*	*war*	wear
word	*worn*	warn	swear
worm	swore	warm	
world		swarm	
worth		wart	
worse		warp	
		dwarf	

Homophones are in italics.

SPELL CHECK 5   ASSESSMENT FOR *R*-INFLUENCED VOWELS

(See page 77.) This assessment is presented in a word recognition format and checks for the recognition of the correct spelling pattern of 20 *r*-influenced words. The Spell Check assesses the short and long *r*-influenced vowel sounds as well as the /ər/ sound. Six homophones are included to assess student knowledge of the spelling patterns that differentiate their word meanings. All of the words assessed have been studied before in Sorts 25 to 30. Photocopy page 77. for all students you wish to participate in the Spell Check. Tell your students to circle the word under each picture that matches the correct spelling pattern.

An alternative way to administer the test is to simply call the words aloud as in a traditional spelling test format. Students would simply number their paper from 1 to 20 while you name the word and use it in a sentence offered below. You may need the sentences to be sure students know which meaning the pictures are targeting, especially for the homophones. Students who score 90% or better on a pretest can move on to other features.

1. **Bird.** A **bird** is a warm-blooded, egg-laying, feathered vertebrate with wings. **Bird.**
2. **Thorn.** A **thorn** is a sharp, spiny point that sticks out of a plant stem and can prick your finger. **Thorn.**
3. **Shirt.** A **shirt** is a piece of clothing worn on the upper part of the body. **Shirt.**
4. **Jar.** A **jar** is a glass container with a wide mouth, usually without handles; used to store things like honey. **Jar.**
5. **Tire.** A **tire** is a covering for a wheel, usually made out of rubber. **Tire.**
6. **Fire.** They learned how to start a **fire** by rubbing two sticks together. **Fire.**
7. **Heart.** Most valentines are in the shape of a **heart. Heart.**
8. **Deer.** A male **deer** grows antlers and is sometimes called a buck. **Deer.**
9. **Horn.** A **horn** is a musical instrument such as a trumpet. **Horn.**
10. **Worm. Worms** are invertebrate animals that often have no arms or legs. **Worms.**
11. **Four.** The number **four** comes after the number three. **Four.**
12. **Chair.** A **chair** is a piece of furniture that makes it possible for people to sit. **Chair.**
13. **First. First** corresponds in order to the number 1. **First.**
14. **Yarn. Yarn** is a long strand of twisted thread made of a fiber such as wool, and is used in weaving or knitting. **Yarn.**
15. **Pliers. Pliers** are a type of tool used for holding, bending, or cutting. **Pliers.**
16. **Pear.** A **pear** is a type of fruit that is eaten like an apple. **Pear.**
17. **Corn. Corn** is a type of grain or cereal plant that bears seeds or kernels on large ears. **Corn.**
18. **Horse.** A **horse** is a large hoofed animal with a shorthaired coat, a long mane, and a long tail; and is used for riding and carrying heavy loads. **Horse.**
19. **Hare.** A **hare** looks like a rabbit with long ears, large hind feet, and legs that are made for jumping. **Hare.**
20. **Fork.** A **fork** is a three- or four-pronged utensil used for serving or eating food. **Fork.**

SORT 25   *ar, are, air*

ar	*are*	*air*
oddball	**care**	**hair**
part	fair	start
harm	pare	chair
wear	sharp	pair
stare	where	dark
square	hare	pear
heart	shark	fare
bear	stair	bare

SORT 26   *er, ear, eer*

er	*ear*	*eer*	*ear = ur*
oddball	**her**		**deer**
hear	**heard**		fear
spear	steer		earth
herd	clear		here
cheer	perch		peer
fern	dear		year
near	learn		germ
clerk	there		term

SORT 27   *ir, ire, ier*

ir	*ire*	*ier*
girl	**fire**	**drier**
third	bird	birth
tire	flier	shirt
fir	whirl	hire
pliers	swirl	thirst
chirp	crier	skirt
their	twirl	wire
dirt	fur	first

SORT 28   *or, ore, oar, w + or*

or	*ore*	*oar*
w + or	form	more
board	**work**	four
horn	store	roar
word	north	shore
soar	world	floor
corn	fork	wore
worm	door	storm
sore	tore	oar

SORT 29 *ur, ure, ur-e*

ur	*ure*	*ur-e*
oddball	**turn**	**sure**
curve	pure	burn
hurt	curl	church
were	nurse	cure
purse	hurl	burst
churn	curse	surf
purr	curb	blurt
lure	urge	

SORT 30   Review of *ar*, Schwa-plus-r, and *or*

ar	*ər*	*or*
jar	earn	thorn
search	warm	hoarse
hard	pearl	horse
worth	core	worn
worst	chore	snore
warn	sir	yarn
spur	score	lurk
march	bore	boar

Spell Check 5   Assessment for *r*-Influenced Vowels

Name _____

1. burd berd bird	2. thorne thorn thourn
3. shirt shert shurt	4. jar jare jaw
5. tier tire tyre	6. fier flyer fire
7. hart heart hairt	8. deer dear dere
9. horn horne hoarn	10. warm worm wurm
11. fore four for	12. chair chayre chare
13. ferst first furst	14. yawn yaun yarn
15. plyers plires pliers	16. pare pair pear
17. coarn corn corne	18. hoarse house horse
19. hair haer hare	20. fourk furk fork

Unit VI   Diphthongs and Other Ambiguous Vowel Sounds

NOTES FOR THE TEACHER

Background and Objectives

Sorts 31 to 35 deal with the spellings of a variety of other vowel sounds that are not influenced by *r* and are neither long nor short. These other vowel sounds usually involve two vowels (like the double *o* in *book* or the *au* in *cause*) or a vowel and a second letter that has some vowel-like qualities. The /l/ and /w/ sounds are examples of consonants that influence the sound of the vowel in an ambiguous way that is difficult to describe (*salt*, *crowd*). Often the influence of the second letter creates a *glide*, where the vowel sound slithers from one sound to another, as in the word *boy*, where the vowel starts out like the vowel sound in *door* but slides into a long *-e* sound at the very end (*bo-ee*). These glides, or diphthongs, can be tricky. Students will:

- Learn the two spellings associated with the sound in *point* and *boy* (*oi* and *oy*)
- Learn the two sounds associated with the *oo* spelling in *soon* and *good*
- Learn the three spellings commonly associated with the sound in *saw, cause,* and *small,* as well as the *o* in *cross* and the *ough* spelling as in *thought* (*aw, au, al, o,* and *ough*)
- Learn the broad *a* spelling in vowels preceded by *w*
- Learn the two spellings associated with the sound in *sound* and *brown* (*ou* and *ow*)

Targeted Learners

The study of diphthongs and other ambiguous vowels is appropriate for students in the late within word pattern stage who have already mastered most of the common and less common short- and long-vowel patterns. Diphthongs and other ambiguous vowels are usually the last vowel patterns to be learned in the within word pattern stage. We place them here, after the *r*-influenced vowels, so that all of the vowel patterns are learned in a planned sequence. However, they could just as easily be studied before *r*-influenced vowels or after the complex consonants presented in the next set of sorts.

Use the Spell Check on page 91 as a pretest to make sure your students need and can do these sorts. Students who spell 90% of the words on the Spell Check correctly may benefit from the study of the more difficult features introduced later in this supplement.

Teaching Tips

In *WTW* we recommend highlighting a new spelling feature by comparing it to what students already know. This is done in Sort 31 where long *-o* is compared to the diphthong *oy*. If you feel that your students need to contrast more familiar short and long sounds to the new sounds in the other sorts you may want to modify the sorts by adding words from the additional lists. For example, you may want to contrast short -*a* with *aw* and *au* in Sort 33 and short -*o* with *ou* and *ow* in Sort 35. These contrasts might be especially helpful for ELLs whose native language does not have these ambiguous sounds. Spanish does have the *oy* sound and spelling pattern but not the *oi*. Listen carefully to hear how students pronounce these words and consider contrasts that might help them sort out the new sounds.

We recommend recycling Sorts 31 to 35 to review all of these similar vowel sounds before the spell check. The review can be a giant pattern sort or a two-step sort that sorts first by sound and then by pattern within categories of sound.

Diphthongs and other ambiguous vowels are not as common as short and long or *r*-influenced vowel patterns, so there are words in each sort that may be unfamiliar to students. This is all right as long as students can read the words and are familiar with the majority of them. These word meanings must be introduced, discussed, and used in meaningful contexts throughout the week. See page 18 for suggested weekly routines to use with these sorts. During word hunts students may find it difficult sometimes to locate additional words with some of these sounds and patterns because they are less common. Hopefully they will discover them in two-syllable words.

Each of the sorts in this series contains approximately 25 words plus two column headers. Key words have been bolded and these should be placed at the top of each column. Oddballs are either high-frequency words whose patterns violate the dominant pattern-to-sound correspondence (e.g., *laugh*) or are words that have an unusual pattern for that particular sound. Some of these patterns form a consistent category of their own. For example, the high-frequency words *should, would,* and *could* have an unusual spelling pattern for that particular sound, but these three words form a small but consistent pattern-to-sound category by themselves.

Many games described in *WTW* can be adapted to these features. Slap Jack and Double Crazy Eights are card games that are particularly appropriate for use with ambiguous spelling patterns. They are described in Chapter 7 of *WTW*.

Literature Connection

If possible, share books and poems that contain some words with the same targeted spelling features. For example, the traditional song *I Wish I Was a Mole in the Ground* (Tashjian, 1941) has many diphthong sounds for *ou* and *ow*, and such books as *Minnie and Moo Go to the Moon* (by Denys Cazet) and *Midnight on the Moon* (by Mary Pope Osborn) contain many examples of *ou, ow,* and *oi*.

SORT 31   LONG -*O, OI, OY*

(See page 86.) The diphthongs in words such as *point* and *boy* spelled with one of two patterns (*oi* or *oy*) offer a reliable letter-sound correspondence. Begin by reading through the words, going over the meanings of any that might need discussion. Identify the two sounds in the words and sort them by sound—words with the familiar long -*o* sound and words with the new sound using the key words as headers. Talk about the patterns under long -*o* but do not sort them further. Then ask students to identify the spelling patterns in the other column and separate the words under the key words *point* and *boy*. Add the pattern headers at this time and then resort again by sound and the new patterns at the same time The words *noise, choice,* and *voice* could be sorted with the *oi* words, or placed as oddballs because of their final *e*.

o	oi		oy	
whole	**point**	moist	**boy***	noise
bowl	join	joint	soy	choice
stole	soil	boil	joy	voice
loan	spoil	coin	toy	
cloak	coil	broil		
choke	foil	oil		

*High-frequency word

Demonstrate, Sort, Check, Reflect, and Extend

Demonstrate, sort, check, reflect, and then **extend** as usual by following the standard weekly routines described on page 18. As you and your students reflect on this sort, help them form generalizations by asking which spelling pattern is used when the /oyee/ sound is at the very end of a word. Which spelling pattern is used when the /oyee/ sound is in the middle of a word? Remind them of the open-syllable patterns *ay, ew, ow, ue,* and *y.*

Additional Words.   mole, role, toil, hoist, ploy, enjoy, decoy

SORT 32   o͞o, o͝o

(See page 87.) Both of these sounds and patterns have been introduced previously (Sorts 12 and 15) but here they are contrasted for the first time. This is a sound sort that compares the long -u sound in words like *soon* and *root* to another back vowel sound in words like *good* and *foot.* All of them are spelled with a double -o. The words *could, would,* and *should* are oddballs because they have the same vowel sound as the words *stood* and *good,* but are spelled differently. Conveniently, *would* and *wood* as well as *root* and *route* are homophones so you can discuss the necessity for having different spelling patterns to reflect their different meanings. Boldface words are the most frequently occurring words in that pattern and could be used as key words to head the columns.

Demonstrate, Sort, Check, Reflect, and Extend

Demonstrate, sort, check, reflect, and then **extend** this word sort by following the standard weekly routines.

o͞o		o͝o		oddball
soon*	tool	**good***	hook	could*
cool	troop	brook	soot	would*
fool	hoop	crook	wool	should*
noon	stool	wood		route
groom	proof	hood		
root	roost	stood		

*High-frequency word; homophones are in italics.

Additional Words.   coop, brood, spool, doom, gloom, spook, zoom, loot, foot, rook, nook

SORT 33   AW, AU, ô

(See page 88.) There are a number of patterns associated with this ambiguous vowel making it difficult for the speller to know which one to use. This pattern sort introduces the reliable correspondences *aw* and *au* as well as the single *o.* The words spelled with a single *o* may be considered short in some dialects, but in others there is a distinct difference (so that *sauce* rhymes with *cross*). Listen to the way your students pronounce these words and discuss possible differences in pronunciation. Before demonstrating the sort, be sure to read and discuss the meanings of the words, especially the asterisked ones. For *vault*, you might refer to Gringots (the bank) in *Harry Potter*. The word *laugh* is an oddball because it has the *au* pattern characteristic of the /aw/ sound, but it has a short -*a* sound instead.

If you decide that this two-pattern sort is too easy for your students, consider bringing in the *ou* words from the next sort to increase the number of pattern contrasts (*bought*, *thought*, *brought*, and so on).

Demonstrate, Sort, Check, Reflect, and Extend

Demonstrate, sort, check, reflect, and then **extend** as usual by following the standard weekly routines previously described. As you and your students reflect on this sort, help them form generalizations by asking: *Is there a spelling pattern that is used more often when the /aw/ sound is at the very end of a word? Is there a spelling pattern that is never used when the /aw/ sound is at the end of a word? Are there any other recurring letter patterns within each category worth noting? Which pattern has more ens or els at the very end of words?* Remind them of what they found with *oy* and *oi*. *Oi* and *au* never occur at the end of a word. *Aw* can come at the end or in the middle.

aw		au		ô	oddball
saw*	law	**cause**	haul	cross	laugh
paws	hawk	caught	haunt	cloth	
straw	crawl	fault	vault	frost	
lawn	dawn	*pause*		song	
claw	shawl	sauce			
draw		taught			

*High-frequency word; homophones are in italics.

Word-O.   *loss, song, lost, lawn*

Additional Words.   *raw, awe, dawn, bawl, fawn, drawn, yawn, sprawl, thaw, flaw, maul, launch, haunch, boss, toss, moss, moth, broth, soft, loft, golf, long, strong*

SORT 34   WA, AL, OU

(See page 89.) Discuss the multiple meanings of *stall* and *watch* as you go over the words in this sort. This sound sort contrasts the broad *a* in words like *wash* and *watch*, the /all/ sound in words like *small* and *salt*, and another /aw/ sound in words like *bought* and *fought*. In some dialects, the words *bought* and *fought* are pronounced more like the short -*o* sound. Either way is fine. There is no one correct pronunciation and English speakers of all dialects must associate their own pronunciation with the same spelling patterns. Even if some students think that *bought, thought,* and *brought* have the same vowel sound as *salt* and *talk,* they can still sort by pattern. Note that two two-syllable words are used—*almost* and *also,* but these are very high-frequency words that students at this level should definitely learn how to read and spell if they do not know already. *Though* is the oddball in this sort.

Demonstrate, Sort, Check, Reflect, and Extend

Demonstrate, sort, check, reflect, and then **extend** as usual by following the standard weekly routines. Watch out for the word *walk.* Students will want to put it with the *wa* words but it does not have the same broad *a* sound as *watch.* Think back with your students to words like *war, warn, work,* and *word* in which the *w* exerted an influence on the vowel that followed. It turns out that short *-a* rarely follows the letter *w* in English (*wax* and *wag* are the only one-syllable words) and the broad *a* is the common sound in CVC patterns. Consider words like *waffle, wander, waddle,* and so on, which also have the broad *a* sound. Some of these words may show up in word hunts.

wa	*al*		*ou*	
watch	**small**	calm	**thought**	though
wash	almost	talk	bought	
wand	also	stalk	brought	
wasp	walk	bald	fought	
swap	stall	chalk	ought	
swat	salt		cough	

Additional Words.   *water, swatch, psalm, palm, halt, talk, sought, trough, though*

SORT 35   *OU, OW*

(See page 90.) This pattern sort contrasts the two major spelling patterns for the /ow/ sound in words like *sound* and *crowd*: *ou* and *ow*. These words should all be familiar to your students, but read and discuss them before demonstrating the sort anyway. Since the *ou* words in the previous sort (Sort 34) were associated with the /aw/ sound, explicitly tell your students that the *ou* pattern in this sort represents the /ow/ sound this time. Oddballs include words with *ou* patterns associated with yet another vowel sound (*tough, rough, through*). You might want to recycle your old long *-o* words with the *ow* pattern from Sort 20 just to keep your students on their toes.

Demonstrate, Sort, Check, Reflect, and Extend

Demonstrate, sort, check, reflect, and then **extend** as usual by following the standard weekly routines previously described. Help your students make generalizations about these pattern-to-sound relationships by asking them to reflect on the preponderance of rhyming words in certain categories. As with *au* and *aw*, *ou* never comes at the end of a word, but *ow* can.

ou		*ow*		oddball
out*	count	**how***	drown	tough
cloud	mouth	down*	frown	rough
round	south	growl	gown	through
ground	couch	clown	plow	
found*	scout	owl	town	
shout		brown*		

*High-frequency word

There are plenty of *ou/ow* words for an additional week and you may want to spend a little more time with this complex sound by adding more of the words listed below and including a contrast that reviews the *ow* spelling of long *-o*.

Word-0.   *found, shout, couch, brown, owl, plow*

Additional Words.   *loud, proud, sound, pound, hound, snout, pout, ouch, foul, mouse, pounce, house, ounce, drought, stout, doubt, now, howl, fowl, prowl, scowl, brow, vow, touch, young, own* (oddballs)

SPELL CHECK 6   ASSESSMENT FOR DIPHTHONGS AND OTHER AMBIGUOUS VOWELS

Grand Sort

Before assessing your students' mastery of the spelling patterns associated with diphthongs and other ambiguous vowel sounds, give them a chance to review. Combine all of the word cards from Sorts 31 to 35. Sort them by sound first, and then by pattern within categories of sound.

Slap Jack, described in *WTW* Chapter 7, can be adapted to review some of the sounds in this unit. The words you can write on cards to create a deck are listed below. All the cards are dealt and two players turn over a card at the same time. If they match by sound (*gown* and *growl*, *draw* and *fought*, or *plow* and *cloud*), the first player that slaps them adds them to his or her hand. If they do not make a sound match (*plow* and *blow* or *mouth* and *bought*) and a player slaps them, the other player gets the pile. Students are required to exercise their attention to sound and ignore the powerful visual pull of the patterns which will sometimes lead them astray!

sound	brown	grown	thought	straw	caught
cloud	plow	blow	bought	lawn	cause
shout	clown	show	brought	claw	fault
mouth	town	shown	fought	drawn	sauce
couch	gown	know	ought	yawn	haunt
scout	growl	flow	cough	hawk	haul
south	drown	crow		crawl	taught
pound	cow	flown		shawl	launch
found	owl	known		raw	vault

The unit assessment is presented in a writing sort format. All of the words assessed have been studied before in these previous sorts. Photocopy and enlarge page 91 for all students you wish to participate in a posttest. Say each word clearly and ask your students to write the word in the box labeled with the correct vowel pattern. For example, if you call the word *calm*, students would write *calm* in the third box labeled with an *al* at the top, because the word *calm* is spelled with an *al* in the middle. If you are grading this Spell Check, consider giving 1 point for writing the word in the correct category and another point for the correct spelling of the entire word.

Call out the words in the following order and use each word in a sentence to make sure your students understand what word you are saying. Say each word once, use it in a sentence, then say it again.

1. crawl	2. chalk	3. growl	4. joy
5. spoil	6. mouth	7. caught	8. point
9. taught	10. draw	11. couch	12. stalk
13. drown	14. brought	15. cloud	16. gown
17. lawn	18. calm	19. haul	20. noise
21. thought	22. rough	23. fault	24. could

Allow time for students to reorganize their words if needed. The words *brought, thought, rough,* and *could* might also be squeezed into the *ou* box because this is a pattern-writing sort. Otherwise, the answer sheet will look like this:

1. *aw*	2. *au*	3. *al*	4. *ow*	5. *ou*	6. *oy*	7. *oi*	8. oddballs
crawl	caught	chalk	growl	mouth	joy	spoil	brought
draw	taught	stalk	drown	couch		point	thought
lawn	haul	calm	gown	cloud		noise	rough
	fault						could

SORT 31   Long -o, -oi, -oy

oi	*oy*	**boy**
point	whole	soil
noise	soy	spoil
join	coil	joy
foil	moist	joint
boil	toy	voice
coin	broil	cloak
choke	oil	stole
choice	loan	bowl

SORT 32 $\overline{oo}$, $\breve{oo}$

$\overline{oo}$	$\breve{oo}$	soon
good	cool	crook
fool	wood	could
noon	groom	hood
root	stood	tool
hook	troop	route
hoop	should	brook
stool	proof	wool
would	soot	roost

SORT 33   *aw, au, ô*

aw	**au**	**saw**
cause	lawn	caught
paws	straw	fault
law	claw	sauce
taught	draw	laugh
haul	pause	song
haunt	hawk	crawl
dawn	cross	vault
shawl	cloth	frost

SORT 34   *wa, al, ou*

wa	*al*	*ou*
watch	small	thought
walk	salt	wash
though	calm	bought
wand	talk	stalk
bald	wasp	fought
swap	chalk	stall
ought	swat	brought
cough	also	almost

SORT 35   *ou, ow*

ou	*ow*	**out**
how	cloud	clown
growl	round	down
tough	ground	brown
owl	found	shout
drown	rough	frown
gown	mouth	plow
south	through	couch
scout	town	count

● Spell Check 6   Assessments for Diphthongs and Other Ambiguous Vowels

Name _____

4. ow	8. oddballs
3. al	7. oi
2. au	6. oy
1. aw	5. ou

Unit VII   Beginning and Ending Complex Consonants and Consonant Clusters

NOTES FOR THE TEACHER

Background and Objectives

Sorts 36 to 42 mark a shift in focus from vowel patterns to consonant patterns. Sorts 36 to 39 target complex consonants at the beginning of words, and Sorts 40 to 42 focus on complex consonants at the ends of words. Shifting focus from vowel patterns back to the beginning of words may cause some initial confusion, but with an increase in orthographic knowledge comes a corresponding increase in flexibility. Because your students have now internalized the vowel patterns studied in the previous sections of this supplement, they are probably reading more difficult text and encountering new features such as silent consonants at the beginning (_knife_, _wrong_, _gnat_) and strange-looking consonant clusters like _tch_ and _dge_ at the ends of words (_catch_, _lodge_). To lead your students to higher levels of word knowledge, these features are worth a few weeks of study. Students will:

- Learn the silent initial consonant spelling patterns: _kn_, _wr_, and _gn_
- Learn to spell the complex triple blends: _scr, str, spr, thr, shr_, and _squ_
- Learn how vowels influence the sound of _g_ and _c_ (hard and soft)
- Learn the roll of final _e_ in _-ce, -ve, -se_, and _-ze._
- Learn the final consonant patterns associated with long and short vowels: ge, _dge_, _ch_, and _tch_

Targeted Learners

The study of complex consonants is appropriate for students in the late within word pattern stage who have already mastered the vowel patterns presented earlier in this supplement. We place them here so that vowel sounds are thoroughly understood before examining how they also affect consonants. As always, we recommend that you assess all of your students with one of the _WTW_ spelling inventories to make sure you are matching your word study instruction to student needs appropriately.

Teaching Tips

Each of the sorts in this series contains 23 or 24 words plus three or four column headers. Key words have been bolded and these should be placed at the top of each column. As always, key words are the most frequently occurring words of that particular spelling pattern. Some oddballs are high-frequency words that violate the dominant pattern-to-sound correspondence. A few of these words may be more difficult than the third- to fourth-grade words previously sorted, so the importance of bringing the meanings of these words to life is paramount, especially for our English Language Learners (ELLs).

The study of complex consonants begins with a look at silent consonants at the beginning of words like _knight_, _wreath_, and _gnat_. This is followed by two sorts that revisit more advanced forms of consonant blends and consonant digraphs, specifically, triple *r*-blends like the *scr, str,* and *spr* (<u>scr</u>een, <u>str</u>ong, <u>spr</u>ing) and triple-letter consonant digraph-plus-*r*-blend combinations like *thr* and *shr* (<u>thr</u>ough, <u>shr</u>ed). Because these triple *r*-blends and digraph-*r*-blend combinations involve that slippery *r* again, you might want to combine Sorts 37 and 38 with some of the *r*-influenced words from Sorts 25 to 30. The study of these triple *r*-blends and digraph-plus-*r*-blend combinations might be accomplished in 1 or 2 weeks depending on your students' previous experience and knowledge. See Chapter 6 in *WTW* for additional suggestions for pacing.

Although Sort 39 (hard and soft *c* and *g*) still focuses on consonants at the beginning of words, hard and soft *c* and *g* are determined by the vowel that follows, so this sort segues nicely into the study of complex consonants at the end of words that are also determined by the vowel sound. Sort 40 shifts the focus to the ends of words and examines words ending in *-ce* versus *-se* as in *peace* versus *please*. Sorts 41 and 42 deal with the complex consonants *tch* and *dge* at the end of words like *match* and *lodge*. This feature continues to bewilder students in the middle to late within word pattern stage who use but confuse *ch* and *tch, ge,* and *dge.* They may spell *pitch,* PICH, or *lodge,* LOGE. Fortunately these consonant patterns are determined by vowel sounds, so students return to familiar word study routines in Sorts 41 and 42 such as sorting words by vowel sounds.

Continue using the same weekly routines described on page 18. The activities section at the end of *WTW* Chapter 6 describes a Jeopardy game for *tch* and *ch.* You can download ready-made card games called Take-A-Card that highlight the silent consonants *gn, kn,* and *wr* and the complex consonants *tch/ch* and *dge/ge* from the *WTW* CD-ROM. Scattergories is another game described on the CD-ROM that could be adapted by using word endings such as *-atch, -itch, -each, -oach, -age, -adge, -edge, -idge, -udge, -ance, -ince, -ove, -ease,* and so forth.

This unit is punctuated by the inclusion of three Spell Checks. Spell Check 7 assesses student mastery of triple *r*-blends and triple digraph-plus-*r*-blend clusters at the beginning of words. Spell Check 8 assesses student mastery of hard and soft *c* and *g* as well as *ce, se,* and *ve* word endings. Spell Check 9 assesses student knowledge of when to use *tch* versus *ch,* and when to use *dge* versus *ge* at the ends of words. You could also use these Spell Checks as a pretest to see if your students truly need each set of sorts.

Literature Connection

If possible, share books, songs, or poems that use some words that contain the targeted spelling feature. *Stone Fox* (by John Reynolds Gardiner) uses many complex consonant blends like *strength, stronger,* and *straight.*

SORT 36   SILENT BEGINNING CONSONANT
KN, WR, GN

(See page 103.) Students in the within word pattern stage will invariably encounter words spelled with silent consonants. Some have already been included in the earlier vowel pattern sorts in this supplement, such as *know* and *knew*; but encounters with silent consonants, up to this point, have been incidental. Sort 36 explicitly lays out three categories of silent consonants for direct instruction. Begin by reading and discussing the words and their meanings. Some students may be totally unfamiliar with words like *wreath, knead,* and *gnaw,* so think about how you will bring those words to life in advance. Oddballs include two homophones (*rap, ring*), to contrast with their silent partners (*wrap, wring*). Other words with homophone mates are *knot, knead, knight,* and *write.* Be sure your students know the correct meaning to associate with these.

Introduce this sort by establishing the headers and key words, or present it as an open sort and let students discover the categories.

kn		wr		gn	oddball
knife	knight	**write**	wren	**gnat**	*rap*
knack	knee	*wrap*	*wring*	gnaw	*ring*
known	kneel	wreck		gnome	
knot	knelt	wrist			
knob	knead	wreath			
knit		wrong			

Homophones are in italics.

Demonstrate, Sort, Check, Reflect, and Extend

Demonstrate, sort, check, reflect, and then **extend** as usual by following the standard weekly routines previously described.

Additional Words. *knapsack, knock, know, knew, knoll, knave, wrack, wraith, wrath, wretch, wreak, wrench, wrought, gnash, gnarl*

SORT 37   TRIPLE *R*-BLENDS *SCR, STR, SPR*

(See page 104.) Students are already familiar with the *s*-blends *sc, st,* and *sp,* so you might want to begin by writing some words on the board to contrast these easier two-letter blends with their more complex three-letter cousins. For example, you might contrast *sc* words like *scott, scare,* and *scat* with some *scr* words in this sort like *scrape* and *scream.* Likewise, you might compare *st* words like *stop, step,* or *star* with some of these *str* words like *strong, straight,* or *string.* Words starting with *sp* (*spot, speech, spit*) might be contrasted with the *spr* words in this sort (*spring, spray, sprout*). Starting in this way will guide your students to look carefully at these beginning consonant clusters and to listen for the presence of the *r* in the triple blends. You might even count the phonemes in two- and three-letter blends by underlining each letter that goes with each sound.

Demonstrate, Sort, Check, Reflect, and Extend

Once your students are accustomed to looking carefully at these blends, introduce the sort with the key words and direct your students' attention to what is the same and what is different among the *scr, str,* and *spr* blends. Then, **demonstrate, sort, check, reflect,** and **extend** as usual by following the standard weekly routines previously described.

scr	*str*		*spr*
screen	**strong**	stripe	**spring**
scram	straight	struck	spray
scrape	strange	strength	sprout
scratch	stretch	stress	spread
scrap	strict	strap	sprain
scream	string	stream	

Additional Words.   *scrub, screw, scrawl, script, scribe, scroll, sprig, sprite, sprawl, spruce, straw, stray, strut, strain, strife, strobe, stride, strewn, stroll, stroke*

SORT 38   CONSONANT DIGRAPHS-PLUS-*R*-BLENDS AND *SQU* (*THR, SHR, SQU*)

(See page 105.) Remind your students that digraphs are two letters that represent one sound. Because the digraphs *th* and *sh* are already familiar to within word pattern spellers, you might begin by contrasting these easier two-letter digraphs with their more complex three-letter digraph-plus-*r*-blends. For example, you might contrast *th* words like *though, thank,* and *thing* with some *thr* words in this sort like *through, three,* and *thrill.* Likewise, you might compare *sh* words like *sheep, shed,* or *shut* with some of these *shr* words like *shrimp, shred,* or *shrink.* You will probably want to contrast the number of phonemes represented in these digraphs and digraph-plus-*r*-blends: *th* represents just one sound whereas *thr* represents two (/th/ + /r/). Starting in this way will guide your students to look carefully at these beginning consonant elements and to listen for the presence of the two sounds in the digraph-plus-*r*-blends (/th/ + /r/; or /sh/ + /r/) and three sounds in the *squ* blend (/s/ + /k/ + /w/). It is a challenge to count the initial phonemes in *squirm* and *squirt.* Do you come up with /s/ + /k/ + /w/? Add the next part of the word and you get /s/ + /k/ + /w/ + /r/—something akin to a quadruple blend because you cannot separate out the vowel before the *r.*

Demonstrate, Sort, Check, Reflect, and Extend

As always, be sure to take the time to read and discuss these words, paying particular attention to the homophones. Word sets like *throw, threw, thrown; shrink, shrank, shrunk* and *squish, squash* present convenient opportunities to work in lessons on verb tense. The meaning of some words may be unfamiliar to your students so you will need to discuss them. You might want to talk about how many of the *squ* words listed here are verbs that suggest "tightening" or a release of air. After bringing these words to life, introduce the keywords, then **demonstrate, sort, check, reflect,** and **extend** as usual by following the standard weekly routines previously described. You simply must read *Shrek* (Stieg, 2002) to your class and make it available for word hunts.

thr		shr		squ	
three*	*threw*	**shred**	shrimp	**square**	squeeze
thrill	*through*	shrink	shrup	squawk	squirt
throw	threat	shrank		squint	squeak
throne		shrunk		squish	squirm
thrown		shriek		squash	

*High-frequency word; homophones are in italics.

Additional Words.   *thrive, thrift, thrust, throng, throat, throb, thrash, thread, thrive, shrew, shrewd, shrug, shrill, shroud, squid, squad, squat, squall, squeal, squire, squelch, squirrel*

● SPELL CHECK 7   ASSESSMENT FOR BEGINNING COMPLEX CONSONANT CLUSTERS

(See page 106.) This assessment is presented in a writing sort format and checks for correct spelling of complex consonant clusters at the beginning of words. All of the 21 words assessed have been studied before in Sorts 37 and 38. Say each word clearly and ask your students to write the word in the box labeled with the complex consonant cluster that matches. If you are grading this Spell Check, give 1 point for writing the word in the correct category and another point for the correct spelling of the entire word. To make it a bit more challenging you can give it in the traditional format and simply ask students to write the words in a list as you call them.

Call out the words in the following order and use each word in a sentence to make sure your students understand what word you mean. There are two homophones (*through* and *threw*) in this assessment, so meaningful sentences are crucial. Say each word once, use it in a sentence, and then say it again.

1. squeeze	**2.** straight	**3.** threw	**4.** spring
5. shrink	**6.** screen	**7.** strong	**8.** spray
9. squirt	**10.** scrape	**11.** through	**12.** shrank
13. scream	**14.** three	**15.** shred	**16.** string
17. sprout	**18.** thrill	**19.** stripe	**20.** scrap

● Allow time for students to reorganize their words if needed. Students may want you to repeat the sentences for the homophones *threw* and *through* to make sure they have them in the right order. Student answer sheets will look like this:

1. *squ*	2. *thr*	3. *shr*	4. *scr*	5. *spr*	6. *str*
squeeze	threw	shrink	screen	spring	straight
squirt	through	shrank	scrape	spray	strong
	three	shred	scream	sprout	string
	thrill		scrap		stripe

SORT 39   HARD AND SOFT *C* AND *G*

(See page 107.) When the sound of *c* is pronounced /k/ and the sound of *g* is pronounced /g/, they are called hard *c* and hard *g*. When the sound of *c* is pronounced /s/ and the sound of *g* is pronounced /j/, they are called soft *c* and soft *g*. The hard sounds of *c* and *g* occur when followed by *a*, *o*, or *u*. The soft sounds of *c* and *g* occur when followed by *e*, *i*, or *y*.

Demonstrate

This "rule" holds up pretty well and students will get a lot of mileage out of knowing it—not only for reading and spelling words in the within word pattern stage, but also for reading and spelling much harder words later on. *Get* and *give* (and *girl*) are oddballs but they occur so frequently they are easy to remember.

● Sort, Check, and Reflect

Be sure to read and discuss the meanings of these words before introducing the sort. Discuss the homophones *gem*, *gym*, *cent*, and *cell*. Even though *sent* and *sell* are not included in this sort, be sure to discuss them and even write them on the board or over-head so that students can see how the homophone partners for *cent* and *cell* are spelled. You might remind students that most homophones are differentiated by their long-vowel pattern, but *cell* and *sell*, *cent* and *sent*, are differentiated by their initial consonant. Also discuss the meaning of the word *gist*, which will likely be unfamiliar to most students.

It is important to sort these words in two ways: (1) by hard and soft consonant sounds at the beginning, and (2) by the vowels that follow the consonant. The first way of sorting teaches students the terminology and shows them how to pay attention to the "softness" or "hardness" of the beginning consonant sound. The second way teaches students to focus on the vowels that follow the consonants. Be sure to have your students sort these words both ways.

To sort by hard and soft consonant sounds, have your students put all the *c* words that start with a /k/ sound in one group and all the *c* words that start with an /s/ sound in another group. Then have students sort all the *g* words that start with a /g/ sound in one group and all the *g* words that start with a /j/ sound in another. After students get the hang of this you can have them sort *c* and *g* words simultaneously, sorting them into two groups corresponding to "hard" and "soft" sounds. The sort will look something like this:

Hard *c*	Soft *c*	Hard *g*	Soft *g*
card	**city**	**gave**	**giant**
code	center	golf	gem
cart	circle	guess	gym
cub	cease	guest	germ
calf	cell	guide	gist
	cent	guilt	
		goose	

To teach students that vowels determine the "hardness" and "softness" of the beginning consonant, have them sort *c* and *g* words according to the vowels that follow them. *C* and *g* words followed by *a, o,* and *u* can be sorted in one group; *c* and *g* words followed by *e, y,* or *i* can be sorted in another group. Again, after they have learned to look for these vowels, students can sort *c* and *g* words by the ensuing vowels simultaneously. Then the sort will look something like this.

Hard			Soft	
card	code	cub	**city**	cease
cart	golf	guess	gym	cell
calf	goose	guest	gist	cent
gave		guide	**giant**	gem
		guilt		germ

Extend

Extend this basic word sort by following the standard weekly routines previously de-scribed. Help your students form generalizations as they reflect on this sort by asking them what vowels follow the hard *c* and the hard *g*, and what vowels follow the soft *c* and soft *g*.

An extension to this lesson is to pull out the words with the silent *u* after the *g*: *guess, guest, guide,* and *guilt*. Write the words on the board and review why they have a hard *g*. Then erase the *u* in each one and read the resulting word: *gess, gest, gide,* and *gilt*. What is the purpose of the silent *u*? It isolates the influence of the vowel that would otherwise make it soft!

Additional Words.   *gain, goof, gulp, gust, gulf, guard, gauge, gene, gyp, gentle, ginger, cinch, cyst, cite, center, cough, cult, cuff*

SORT 40   FINAL *E*: *-CE, -VE, -SE, -ZE*

(See page 108.) In this sort, different word endings that include a final *e* will be compared to focus students' attention to the sound of the final consonant, particularly the /s/ sound of *ce* endings and the /z/ sound of *se*. Words ending in *ve* and *ze* are included for contrast and to teach students that all English words that end in *v* also end in *e* (except *LUV* diapers!) and many words that end in *z* also have an *e* added.

Demonstrate, Sort, Check, and Reflect

This is a straightforward pattern sort and might be introduced as an open sort. Before introducing it, read and discuss the words, paying particular attention to the homophones *piece* and *peace*. Ask if anyone knows of another word that sounds just like *sense* that has a different meaning, and hence, a different spelling pattern (*since* and *cents*). There are two words included with the *se* word endings that do not have the /z/ sound at the end like the others do (*loose, sense*). Go ahead and sort these two with the *se* endings because this is a pattern sort, but see if your students can spot them. Discuss the spelling and meaning of the word *loose* in contrast to the word *lose*, which does end in a /z/ sound spelled with the *se* ending. To help them remember the spelling of *loose*, ask students if they know any words that rhyme with *loose*. Write down their brainstorms under the word *loose*: *goose, moose,* and *caboose* may be volunteered and a quick study of their sound and spelling pattern will help students differentiate *loose* from *lose*.

-ce		-ve		-se		-ze
chance	*piece*	**move**	solve	**please***	loose**	**freeze**
prince	*peace*	leave	prove	tease	house**	seize
dance	bounce	twelve	shove	choose		snooze
fence	glance	glove		cheese		

*High-frequency word
**Oddball by sound of ending

Extend

An extension to this sort is to present students with a list of words that end with *-se* and contrast them with the same words without an *e*: *tease-teas, moose-moos, dense-dens, tense-tens, please-pleas*. The words that just end in *s* are plurals. Sometimes the *e* helps us know that we are not talking about a plural, but a different word. There are not a lot of these but they are interesting!

Additional Words.   *ounce, pounce, hence, force, once, niece, truce, weave, curve, sleeve, nerve, serve, house, mouse, dense, tense, false, moose, goose, purse, rinse, verse, bruise, poise, raise, gauze, sneeze, breeze, maize, wheeze, bronze, gauze*

SPELL CHECK 8 ASSESSMENT FOR HARD AND SOFT *C* AND *G* AND WORD ENDINGS *-CE*, *-SE*, *-VE*

(See page 109.) This assessment is presented in a writing sort format and checks for correct spelling of hard and soft *c* and *g* at the beginning of words and the word endings *ce*, *se*, and *ve*. All of the 20 words assessed have been sorted in Sorts 39 and 40. Copy and enlarge page 109 for all students you wish to participate in the Spell Check (or use a traditional format). Say each word clearly and ask your students to write the word in the box labeled with the correct beginning consonant sound or correct word ending. For example, if you call the word *freeze*, students would write *freeze* in the sixth box labeled with *-ze*. If you are grading this Spell Check, give 1 point for writing the word in the correct category and another point for the correct spelling of the entire word.

Call out the words in the order presented below, and use each word in a sentence to make sure your students understand what word you mean. There are two homophones included in this assessment (*gym* and *peace*), so meaningful sentences are critical. Say each word once, use it in a sentence, and then say it again.

1. twelve	**2.** calf	**3.** please	**4.** city
5. freeze	**6.** guess	**7.** leave	**8.** giant
9. loose	**10.** peace	**11.** seize	**12.** card
13. cheese	**14.** glove	**15.** dance	**16.** choose
17. gym	**18.** fence	**19.** gave	**20.** prove

Allow time for students to reorganize their words if needed. Students may want you to repeat the sentences for the homophones *peace* and *gym* to make sure they have spelled the right one. Student answer sheets will look like this:

1. Hard *c* or *g*	2. Soft *c* or *g*	3. *-ce*	4. *-se*	5. *-ve*	6. *-ze*
calf	city	peace	please	twelve	freeze
guess	giant	dance	loose	leave	seize
card	gym	fence	cheese	glove	
gave			choose	prove	

SORT 41 *DGE, GE*

(See page 110.) In single-syllable short-vowel words that end with a /j/ sound, the final phoneme is spelled *dge (lodge, ledge, bridge, badge, fudge)*. Long vowels, ambiguous vowels, and the letters *r, n,* and *l* precede the *ge* spelling (*cage, lounge, large, binge, bulge*). This stable state of affairs calls for a good old-fashioned sound sort. Sort by vowel sound—short versus long versus vowel plus *r, l,* or *n*.

Demonstrate, Sort, Check, and Reflect

Help your students form generalizations by prompting them to articulate what is the same and what is different about words within and across categories. **Compare,** and then, **declare.**

Extend

At this point you may want to work with your students to create a chart of the different roles that final *e* plays: It works as a vowel marker (CVCe), it often follows final *c, s, v,* and *z*, and it marks soft *g* and *c*. It also marks a voiced *th* in words like *bathe, breathe, clothe,* and *teethe.* Contrast those with the same words without the *e: bath, breath, cloth, teeth.*

Look for the *WTW* CD-ROM and check out the Take-A-Card game that features complex consonants *dge* and *ge.*

dge		ge		r, l, or n + ge	
edge	bridge	**age**		**large**	surge
badge	ledge	stage		charge	plunge
ridge	dodge	rage		sponge	
fudge	hedge	cage		bulge	
judge	pledge	huge		range	
lodge				change	

Additional Words. *wage, sage, luge, hedge, wedge, budge, smudge, trudge, grudge, forge, gorge, nudge, orange, gauge, hinge, lounge, merge*

SORT 42   *TCH, CH*

Demonstrate, Sort, Check, and Reflect

(See page 111.) The same principle illustrated in Sort 41 works for the /ch/ sound at the end of words. When you hear a short-vowel sound, use *tch,* unless you hear an *r, l,* or *n* before the final /ch/, in which case you use *ch.* When you hear a long-vowel sound, always use *ch.* The high-frequency words *rich, much, which,* and *such* are exceptions and must be remembered.

Begin with a pattern sort first (*tch, ch*) and then sort the *ch* group by vowel sounds. Either way gets you to this:

Note: *Coach, beach, reach,* and *which* have been used in earlier sorts.

tch		ch		r, l, n + ch		oddball
catch	fetch	**reach**	beach	**lunch**	branch	*which**
witch	match	roach	speech	torch	crunch	rich
pitch	hutch	screech		gulch	porch	much*
sketch	switch	coach		bench		

*High-frequency words; homophones are in italics.

Extend

During a word hunt students might find *touch, couch,* or *pouch.* These might be considered oddballs but if the generalization changes to one vowel before *tch* and two vowels before *ch,* they would fit. The Jeopardy game show in Chapter 6 of *WTW* is set up to review words that end in *ch.*

Additional Words. *ditch, snitch, blotch, stitch, swatch, glitch, crutch, beech, mooch, pooch, smooch, touch, couch, pouch, grouch, poach, hunch, munch, punch, pinch, search, birch, mulch, French*

SPELL CHECK 9   ASSESSMENT FOR COMPLEX CONSONANT CLUSTERS *DGE/GE* AND *TCH/CH*

(See page 112.) Review both Sorts 41 and 42 by sorting them by sound and pattern. Students should see that *tch* and *dge* are associated with short vowels while *ch* and *ge* go with long vowels. Words where the middle vowel is followed by *r, l,* or *n* work similarly.

This writing sort checks for correct spelling of the complex consonants *dge, ge, tch,* and *ch* at the end of words. All of the 20 words assessed have been sorted in Sorts 39 and 40. Say each word clearly and ask your students to write the word in one of the boxes labeled *Short Vowels, Long Vowels,* or *Vowel + r, l,* or *n*. For example, if you call the word *lodge,* students would write *lodge* in the first box labeled *Short Vowels,* because the word *lodge* is a short-vowel word so it takes the *dge* spelling. If you are grading this Spell Check, give 1 point for writing the word in the correct category and another point for the correct spelling of the entire word.

Call out the words in the following order and use each word in a sentence to make sure your students understand what word you mean. Say each word once, use it in a sentence, and then say it again. Feel free to add some exceptions if you like; students can write them across the bottom.

1. change	2. catch	3. stage	4. badge
5. bench	6. screech	7. rage	8. judge
9. gulch	10. pitch	11. cage	12. porch
13. charge	14. crunch	15. roach	16. lodge
17. coach	18. pledge	19. sketch	20. strange

Allow time for students to reorganize their words if needed. Answer sheets will look like this:

1. Short Vowels		2. Long Vowels		3. Vowel + *r, l,* or *n*	
catch	lodge	stage	roach	change	charge
badge	pledge	screech	coach	bench	crunch
judge	sketch	rage		gulch	strange
pitch		cage		porch	

SORT 36   Silent Beginning Consonant *kn*, *wr*, *gn*

kn	*wr*	*gn*
knife	**write**	**gnat**
rap	knack	wreck
known	wrist	knot
gnaw	ring	wrap
knob	knit	wren
wrong	knight	knead
kneel	knelt	knee
wreath	wring	gnome

SORT 37   Triple *r*-Blends *scr, str, spr*

scr	*str*	*spr*
screen	**strong**	**spring**
strange	spray	scram
sprain	strap	strict
stress	scream	scrap
sprout	scrape	string
stripe	struck	spread
scratch	stream	straight
stretch	strength	

SORT 38   Consonant Digraphs-plus-r-Blends and *squ* (*thr, shr, squ*)

thr	*shr*	*squ*
three	shred	square
shrink	throw	throne
squint	threw	shrank
through	squish	thrown
squash	shriek	squeeze
thrill	shrimp	squirt
squeak	threat	squirm
shrub	squawk	shrunk

Spell Check 7   Assessment for Beginning Complex Consonant Clusters

Name _____

3. shr

6. str

2. thr

5. spr

1. squ

4. scr

SORT 39   Hard and Soft c and g

Soft *c*	Hard *c*	Soft *g*
Hard *g*	city	card
giant	gave	cease
guilt	code	gem
gym	golf	goose
cart	guess	cell
cub	germ	guest
cent	calf	guide
gist	circle	center

SORT 40   Final *e*: *-ce, -ve, -se, -ze*

-ce	-ve	-se	-ze
chance	**move**		**please**
freeze	tease		leave
glove	choose		dance
fence	shove		loose
glance	piece		cheese
peace	prince		solve
bounce	prove		house
snooze	twelve		seize

Spell Check 8   Assessment for Hard and Soft *c* and *g*
and Word Endings -*ce*, -*se*, -*ve*

Name _____

1. **Hard c or g**

2. **Soft c or g**

3. **-ce**

4. **-se**

5. **-ve**

6. **-ze**

SORT 41   *dge, ge*

dge	ge	r, l, n + ge
edge	**age**	**large**
badge	stage	charge
range	ridge	rage
cage	pledge	bulge
lodge	fudge	huge
change	judge	bridge
ledge	sponge	dodge
hedge	plunge	surge

SORT 42   *tch, ch*

tch	*ch*	*r, l, n + ch*
catch	**reach**	**lunch**
coach	bench	witch
pitch	beach	torch
gulch	speech	which
sketch	screech	roach
fetch	match	branch
porch	crunch	hutch
rich	switch	much

Spell Check 9   Assessment for Complex Consonant Clusters *dge/ge* and *tch/ch*

Name _____

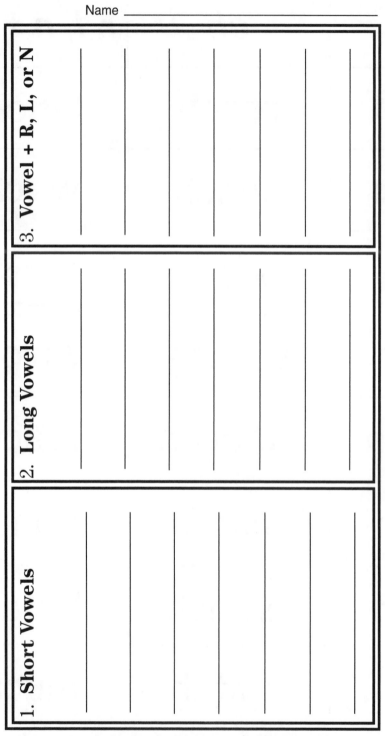

1. Short Vowels

2. Long Vowels

3. Vowel + R, L, or N

Unit VIII High-Frequency Words and Contractions

NOTES FOR THE TEACHER

Background and Objectives

Sorts 43 and 44 take us on a detour into the world of high-frequency words and contractions. Up to this point we have included phonetically irregular high-frequency words in word sorts as oddballs; but there are also some words that students need to write frequently that have not been heretofore included in these weekly lessons. An example of this is the word *because*, which students often spell in their own inventions as BECUZ, BECALZ, or BECAWS. Sort 43 targets many of the high-frequency words that start with the unaccented syllable *be-* (*because*, *believe*, *behind*) and the unaccented syllable *a-* (*again*, *about*, *across*).

Sort 44 focuses on some high-frequency contractions, words that collapse two or more words by removing some letters and replacing them with an apostrophe. Students need to understand how contractions work so they know where to put the apostrophe when they write, and so they can understand the meaning of contractions when they read. Easier contractions were examined in the letter name-alphabetic supplement (*I'm*, *he's*, *she'll*). In Sort 44 we examine more advanced contractions distilled from the combination of adverbs (*where*, *there*, *here*), relative pronouns (*this*, *that*, *who*, *what*), and the like, with helping verbs (*is*, *have*, *will*). Sort 44 presents contractions in groups: the *not* group, the *is* group, the *have* group, and the *will* group. The objective is for students to learn that the apostrophe marks the spot where the letters were removed. Follow the standard weekly routines for word sorts as described in previous sorts.

In addition to the sorting activities recommended throughout this supplement, we suggest that you follow our guidelines for the study of high-frequency words as outlined in Chapter 6 in *WTW*. To summarize, the routine we suggest there includes: (1) discussing each word to identify trouble spots as well as familiar chunks, (2) using a self-corrected pretest, followed by (3) the self-study method (look, say, write, and check), and (4) spell checks.

Targeted Learners

These sorts can be used at any time but because they require students to know how to spell the various vowel patterns in the second syllable of the high-frequency words and the first part of the contractions, we have included them here at the end of the within word pattern stage. Students in the syllables and affixes stage might also benefit from these sorts. As always, the Spell Checks can be used to determine who needs to work with these words.

Teaching Tips

To assess students' mastery of these high-frequency words and contractions, ask them to spell, read, and write the words. Spell Check 10 assesses students' knowledge of high-frequency words in a cloze format using antonyms and synonyms. Spell Check 11 assesses student mastery of more advanced contractions with another cloze procedure in which students write the contraction in the blank provided.

SORT 43   HIGH-FREQUENCY WORDS STARTING WITH A- AND *BE-*

(See page 117.) Sort 43 targets high-frequency words that start with an unaccented syllable. Because the first syllable is unaccented or unstressed, the vowel is reduced to a schwa(e) or an /uh/ sound as in "uh-bove" for *above*, and "buh-cause" for *because*. Fortunately the vowels in the accented or stressed syllable sound and look more familiar—the *way* of *away* and the *fraid* of *afraid* are spelled with the familiar CVV and CVVC long-vowel patterns studied earlier. The same phenomena exists in the "buh" group and the second syllable is sometimes a complete word: the *side* in *beside,* or the *long* in *belong,* for example. It is important to guide your students to recognize what they already know in these high-frequency two-syllable words to move them into the next level of word study where they will examine syllables and affixes in detail.

Demonstrate, Sort, Check, and Reflect

Prepare a set of words to use for teacher-directed modeling. You might make a transparency to cut apart and model sorting on the overhead projector. Display the words and begin by asking the students to read over them to see if there are any they do not know or understand. Because most of these words are adverbs, prepositions, conjunctions, or abstract verbs, they are hard to discuss. Their meaning is not concrete. To get the conversation going you might find all the words having to do with "location" such as *above, below, ahead,* and *behind.* Or, ask students to find some words that could describe a person (*afraid, alive, asleep*). After discussing the words, ask for ideas about how they could be sorted. Students are likely to suggest the beginning syllable so put up the headers.

After sorting all the *a-* words together and all the *be-* words together, read through all the words in a single column. You might want to clap to the rhythm of syllable stress and talk about how the second syllable is accented and the first syllable has an /uh/ sound. Students may argue that they say a long -*a* or -*e* in the first syllable as they read the words. Suggest that they use the word in a sentence where they are more likely to say the word naturally. Explain that accenting the first syllable is a good strategy for remembering how to spell the word. Here is the sort:

a-		*be-*	
away*	alive	before*	beyond
ago	along	because*	become
again*	above	begin	beside
ahead	across	belong	believe
around	afraid	between	below
about*	asleep	behind	began

*High-frequency word

Extend

After your students have sorted their own word cards and have recorded them in their word study notebooks, ask them to underline the second syllable of words that are words by themselves. You can introduce *base word* as a term to describe these words. Here is a list of words that contain words in their second syllable.

a*go*, a*way*, a*round*, a*live*, a*cross*, a*sleep*
be*cause*, be*long*, be*come*, be*side*, be*low*, be*fore*

SPELL CHECK 10   ASSESSMENT FOR HIGH-FREQUENCY WORDS STARTING WITH *A-* AND *BE-*

(See page 118.) This assessment is presented in a cloze format and students must recall 10 high-frequency words that will complete each sentence and write them correctly in the blanks provided. The first five words are prompted by an antonym (opposite) clue in a cloze sentence format. The second five words are prompted by a synonym or definition in a cloze sentence format. If you are grading this assessment, give 1 point for the correct word choice and another point for its correct spelling. The sentences, and their answers, are as follows:

Antonym Cloze

1. The opposite of *above* is (*below*).
2. The opposite of *to end* is (*begin*).
3. The opposite of *awake* is (*asleep*).
4. The opposite of *ahead* is (*behind*).
5. The opposite of *dead* is (*alive*).

Synonym Cloze

6. Another word for *scared* is (*afraid*).
7. To do something *one more time* is to do it (*again*).
8. To go *in front* is to go (*before*).
9. To *get from one side of the street to the other*, you must go (*across*).
10. If I *trust* that you are telling me the *truth*, I (*believe*) you.

SORT 44   CONTRACTIONS

(See page 119.) Sort 44 presents 23 contractions in groups: the *not* group, the *is* group, the *have* group, and the *will* group. These words are boldfaced to be used as key words or column headers. The objective is for students to learn that the apostrophe marks the spot where the letters were removed.

Demonstrate, Sort, Check, and Reflect

Display the headers *not, is, have,* and *will*. Tell your students that contractions are like compound words with one or more letters removed. Use your finger to cover the *o* in the word *not* and explain that if you took the *o* out of *not*, you could put an apostrophe there instead to mark the place where you removed the letter. Put the word *couldn't* under the header *not* and ask a student to show you where the *o* was removed. Use the same procedure for *is*. Cover up the *i* and explain how you could take a shortcut in writing by removing the *i* and putting an apostrophe in its place. Put the word *who's* under the header *is* and ask someone to show you where the *i* was removed. The words *have* and *will* are a bit more complicated, because the first two letters are removed instead of just the vowel, but you can use the same procedure. What is important is for students to see that there is a predictable pattern in the way the words are spelled. Use both the uncontracted form and the contracted form in sentences and encourage students to do the same: *I could not understand the directions. I couldn't understand the directions.*

not	is	have	will
couldn't	who's	could've	they'll
wouldn't	there's	would've	that'll
aren't	here's	should've	this'll
weren't	where's	might've	who'll
don't	what's		she'll
doesn't			he'll
hasn't			you'll

Extend

You may want to have students write sentences using contractions as a word study notebook activity for this week. You might also require them to write out the expanded form of each contraction and underline the letters that are omitted: *could + n<u>o</u>t = couldn't, he + <u>wi</u>ll = he'll.*

Word hunts will turn up other families of contractions like *I'd* (*I would*) and *we're* (*we were*). Challenge the students to write out the expanded form of the constituent parts to discover how the contraction is constructed.

Matching games like Memory or Concentration work well as a review of contractions. Write the contraction on one card and the expanded form on the other.

See if your students can apply their skill with apostrophes to read dialect dialogue in books like *The Talking Eggs* (by Roger D. San Souci), or *Pink and Say* (by Patricia Polacco). Both of these books make heavy use of apostrophes to represent dialect.

SPELL CHECK 11   ASSESSMENT FOR CONTRACTIONS

(See page 120.) In this assessment, students read a sentence that contains two underlined words that could be combined and written as a contraction. Students simply write the contraction in the space provided. If you are grading this assessment, each answer is worth 1 point. The sentences and answers are as follows:

1. <u>They will</u> come to my house for dinner. (*They'll*)
2. <u>Who is</u> going to the party? (*Who's*)
3. She <u>could have</u> won the prize if she had signed her name. (*could've*)
4. They <u>are not</u> the ones who did it. (*aren't*)
5. <u>Here is</u> the work that you missed. (*Here's*)
6. You <u>should not</u> forget your homework. (*shouldn't*)
7. I <u>might have</u> done it differently if I had thought about it. (*might've*)
8. "<u>Who will</u> help me sow the wheat?" asked the Little Red Hen. (*Who'll*)
9. <u>What is</u> five plus three? (*What's*)
10. He <u>does not</u> have enough money to go to the movies. (*doesn't*)

SORT 43   High-Frequency Words Starting with *a-* and *be-*

a-	*be-*	away
before	again	because
ago	between	around
begin	believe	about
alive	become	beyond
ahead	beside	across
below	asleep	afraid
began	behind	above
along		

Spell Check 10   Assessment for High-Frequency Words Starting with *a-* and *be-*

Name _____

Antonym Cloze

1. The opposite of *above* is _____.

2. The opposite of *to end* is _____.

3. The opposite of *awake* is _____.

4. The opposite of *ahead* is _____.

5. The opposite of *dead* is _____.

Synonym Cloze

6. Another word for *scared* is _____.

7. To do something *one more time* is to do it _____.

8. To go *in front* is to go _____.

9. To *get from one side of the street to the other,* you must go _____.

10. If I *trust* that you are telling me the *truth,* I _____ you.

SORT 44   Contractions

not	*is*	*have*
will	couldn't	who's
could've	they'll	wouldn't
there's	would've	that'll
aren't	here's	should've
this'll	weren't	where's
might've	she'll	doesn't
he'll	hasn't	you'll
don't	what's	who'll

Spell Check 11   Contractions

Name _____

Write the contraction for the underlined words

1. <u>They will</u> come to my house for dinner. _____

2. <u>Who is</u> going to the party? _____

3. She <u>could have</u> won the prize if she had signed her name. _____

4. They <u>are not</u> the ones who did it. _____

5. <u>Here is</u> the work that you missed. _____

6. You <u>should not</u> forget your homework. _____

7. I <u>might have</u> done it differently if I had thought about it. _____

8. "<u>Who will</u> help me sow the wheat?" asked the Little Red Hen. _____

9. <u>What is</u> five plus three? _____

10. He <u>does not</u> have enough money to go to the movies. _____

Unit IX   Inflectional Endings for Plural and Past Tense

NOTES FOR THE TEACHER

Background and Objectives

Although issues of changing the base word to accommodate plural and past tense endings are more suitably addressed in the next stage of word knowledge, the syllables and affixes stage, it is important for students in the late within word pattern stage to acquire a conceptual understanding of the plural endings *s* and *es*, and of the past tense *ed*, as meaning units that can be added to base words to indicate number or tense. Students in the late within word pattern stage may still spell these inflectional endings phonetically, as in BEACHIS for *beaches*, or JUMPT for *jumped*. Although students may use these grammatical forms correctly in their speech, they are not aware of them as orthographic meaning units or morphemes in print. Because late within word pattern spellers are reading and writing many words with inflectional endings, it is fitting that they learn the conventional spelling of the two most frequently occurring inflectional endings, plurals and past tense. Changes to the base word to accommodate these endings, such as consonant doubling, dropping the final *e*, or changing the *y* to *i*, will not be addressed here. These more complicated conventions are addressed in the next *WTW* book on sorts for spellers in the beginning syllables and affixes stage. Students will:

- Learn when to use the -*s* and -*es* inflected endings without changes to the base words
- Distinguish between the three sounds of the inflected -*ed* ending (-*t*, -*d*, -*id*) and understand that all are spelled the same
- Spell words with -*ed* added without changes to the base word

Targeted Learners

This sort is for students in the late within word pattern stage who can already spell the many different spelling patterns in the base words. This sort can also be used with students in the early syllables and affixes stage as an introduction to inflected endings.

Teaching Tips

Follow the standard weekly routines suggested for previous sorts. Word hunts will turn up many words for both *s* and *ed*. A collection of *ed* words will include many that double and drop the *e* before adding the ending. These might be used to introduce the rules that govern such changes.

SORT 45   PLURAL ENDINGS *S* AND *ES*

(See page 125.) The letter *s* or *es* is added to nouns to indicate "more than one," but is also added to verbs (*walk, walks*). The inflectional endings *s* and *es* are stable and are always spelled the same way regardless of pronunciation. Students need to be shown how this works. Most of the 25 words presented in Sort 45 have been presented in earlier sorts in this supplement in the singular form. As a result, it will be easy for students to find and underline the base word in these inflected forms.

Introduce the idea of a base word by writing *wishes, wished,* and *wishing* on the board. Underline *wish* in each word and explain that this is the *base word* to which endings can be added. Pass out the student sorts and ask them to underline the base word before they even cut them up. After students have underlined the base word, discuss what is left over—the *s* or *es*. Tell your students that adding an *s* or *es* to a base word tells us there is more than one. You may need to elaborate on this point by comparing 1 inch to 2 inches; one girl to two girls, and so on. Remind your students that they have sorted most of these words in the singular form in an earlier sort.

Once your students have underlined the base word and they understand that the *s* or *es* added to the end of the base word indicates more than one, ask them to sort their word cards by their plural endings—*s* or *es*. They will need to be careful with words like *eyes*, by paying attention to whether the *e* is part of the base word or part of the ending. This sort should result in two columns that look like this:

+ *s*		+ *es*	
eyes	badges	inches	glasses
plants		stitches	dresses
pieces		boxes	lunches
places		taxes	flashes
pages		bushes	coaches
girls		dishes	speeches
months		wishes	bosses
house		classes	riches

Ask your students: *How do you know when to add* s *and when to add* es? After taking on a few hypotheses for discussion, have your students sort the +*es* group by the final letter(s) of the base word, then ask that question again. Is there a reoccurring pattern in the base word of the +*es* group? They should notice that all of the base words end in *sh, ch, s,* or *x*. If students volunteer the final letter *h* instead of *sh* or *ch*, direct their attention to the word *month* in the +*s* column, then ask them to revise the hypothesis.

sh	*ch*	*ss*	*x*
bushes	inches	classes	boxes
dishes	stitches	glasses	taxes
wishes	lunches	bosses	
flashes	coaches	dresses	
	speeches		
	riches		

Demonstrate, Sort, Check, Reflect, and Extend

Demonstrate, sort, check, reflect, and **extend** as usual by following the standard weekly routines previously described.

SORT 46   THREE SOUNDS OF THE PAST TENSE *ED*

(See page 126.) The easiest way to build a conceptual understanding of *ed* as an invariant orthographic unit that tells us that something has already happened in the past is to have students categorize words with -*ed* endings by their ending sounds. Having students sort words with various *ed* sounds leads them to the realization that no matter how we pronounce it, we primarily use *ed* to indicate that an event has happened in the past. In this sort, students sort words ending in *ed* by sound, then they circle the part that tells that the event already occurred in the past. The point of Sort 46 is to introduce students to the invariance of the past tense morpheme *ed*, regardless of how it sounds.

If your students have been in the within word pattern spelling group throughout this book and they have worked with you using the previous sorts, they may recognize just about every one of these words because they have seen them before without the *ed* ending. Tell your students that they are studying these words again because they have all been changed to the past tense by adding an *ed* to the *base word*. Remind them that they talked about base words in the last sort. It is important that you spend some time discussing the concept of past versus present tense by using some of the words in this sort in contrasting sentences with and without the *ed*. For example, you might play Yesterday and Today with the words in this sort. To play this game, choose a word from the sort, take off the *ed*, and then use the base word in a sentence using the present tense for *today*. With the word *walked*, for example, you could take off the *ed* and generate the sentence, "Today I will walk to my yoga class." Next, put the *ed* back on and say, "Yesterday, I walked to my yoga class."

Demonstrate, Sort, Check, and Reflect

Begin with a teacher-directed sound sort. Pull out the key words *prayed, waited*, and *picked.* Say each one with an emphasis on the last sound. Ask your students if they sound the same. Model how to sort several more, each time comparing the word to the key word. Involve the students in sorting the rest of the words, either as a group or individually with their own set of words. Expect for some students to struggle a bit with this sort. After sorting, read down each column, emphasizing the ending and ask students what sound they hear in each word. Display the headers /d/, /id/, and /t/ and tell your students that the letters in the middle of the slash marks indicate the final sound in these words: Some words end in a /d/ sound; in others, the *ed* forms a second syllable and the second syllable sounds like /id/. Some words end in a /t/ sound. The sort will look like this:

/d/		/id/		/t/	
prayed	turned	**waited**	started	**picked**	missed
rained	mailed	loaded	twisted	jumped	passed
snowed	cleaned	needed	handed	walked	dressed
screamed	yelled	melted	dusted	bumped	asked

Help your students reflect on this sort by calling on students to summarize what they learned. Hopefully, they all will learn that the past tense morpheme *ed* is always spelled *ed* no matter how it sounds.

Extend

Extend this sort further by having your students go on a word hunt for other words ending in *ed*. Ask them to add these words to their word study notebooks in the proper columns. *Good Hunting, Blue Sky* (by Peggy Parish) is chock full of *ed* words!

You might want to explore with your students why there are three different sounds for the *-ed* ending. Start by looking at the base words of those that end in /id/. They already end with either a *t* or a *d*. Our mouth will not let us add another /d/ or /t/ without putting a vowel between them. After examining the other base words, students can find that each sound follows particular letters consistently. *S, k, and p* are followed by /t/ (all are unvoiced by the way), and *n, m, and l* (voiced sounds) are followed by /d/. Words that turn up in a word hunt can be added to extend this finding.

SPELL CHECK 12   BASE WORD + INFLECTION: PLURAL AND PAST TENSE ENDINGS

(See page 127.) The assessment for plural and past tense endings is conducted in a cloze sentence format. Students read a sentence that contains an underlined word and then complete the sentence by filling in the blank with the proper inflection. The Spell Check for plurals requires students to change the underlined word from the singular to the plural form by adding an *s* or *es*. Students write the inflected word in the blank provided. The Spell Check for past tense requires students to change the underlined word from the present tense to the past tense by adding *ed*. Students write the inflected form of the word in the blank provided.

Tell students to read each sentence carefully and look for the underlined word. Tell them to complete each sentence by changing the underlined word to the plural form or past tense and writing it on the blank provided. Each answer is worth 1 point. There are 10 plurals and 10 past tense items. The sentences and answers may be found below:

Plural Check (Based on Sort 45)

1. I have one <u>plant </u>but she has two (*plants*).
2. My brother's <u>class</u> has two gym (*classes*) on Fridays.
3. Each new <u>month</u> gets us closer to the (*months*) ahead.
4. She needed a new <u>dress</u> but she shouldn't have bought five new (*dresses*)!
5. The treasure hunt took them from <u>place</u> to <u>place</u> until they had been to all of the (*places*) they could possibly go.
6. I cannot see you as clearly with one <u>eye</u> shut as I can with both (*eyes*) open.
7. We moved from <u>house</u> to <u>house</u> until we had lived in five different (*houses*).
8. He grew <u>inch</u> by <u>inch</u> until he had grown three (*inches*).
9. One <u>box</u> was red and another <u>box</u> was blue, but all of the (*boxes*) had ribbons.
10. He hid behind one <u>bush</u> then ran to the (*bushes*) on the other side of the lawn.

Past Tense Check (Based on Sort 46)

1. Her teacher told her to <u>ask</u> nicely so she (*asked*) as nicely as she could.
2. It might <u>rain</u> again today. Last night it (*rained*) two inches.
3. I hope it will <u>snow</u> tonight. Last year it (*snowed*) on Valentine's Day.
4. The snow will <u>melt</u> when the sun comes out. Last time it (*melted*) before noon.
5. He can <u>jump</u> higher than anyone on the team. He (*jumped*) seven feet at the last meet.
6. She can really <u>yell</u> loudly. She (*yelled*) so much at the game that she lost her voice.
7. The girls won't <u>start</u> in the race this week. Last week they (*started*) before the gun went off.
8. The workers <u>pick</u> apples all fall. Last fall they (*picked*) 2,000 barrels of apples.
9. They <u>load</u> the apples onto trucks. Last year they (*loaded*) 500 trucks.
10. Mrs. Smith <u>walks</u> every day. Last week she (*walked*) 10 miles.

SORT 45   Plural Endings *s* and *es*

+s	+es	dishes
eyes	inches	stitches
boxes	bushes	places
pages	wishes	classes
glasses	riches	dresses
girls	taxes	houses
bosses	coaches	flashes
speeches	months	badges
pieces	plants	lunches

SORT 46   Three Sounds of the Past Tense *ed*

/d/	/id/	/t/
prayed	**waited**	**picked**
jumped	loaded	rained
needed	snowed	walked
screamed	melted	bumped
turned	missed	started
passed	mailed	twisted
cleaned	handed	dressed
dusted	yelled	asked

● Spell Check 12   Part I: Base Word + Inflection: Plurals (Based on Sort 45)

Name _____

*Read each sentence carefully and look for the underlined word. Complete each sentence by changing the underlined word to the **plural form**. Write the **plural form** of the word in the blank provided.*

1. I have one <u>plant</u> but she has two _____.

2. My brother's <u>class</u> has two gym _____ on Fridays.

3. Each new <u>month</u> gets us closer to the _____ ahead.

4. She needed a new <u>dress</u> but she shouldn't have bought five new _____!

5. The treasure hunt took them from <u>place</u> to <u>place</u> until they had been to all of the _____ they could possibly go.

6. I cannot see you as clearly with one <u>eye</u> shut as I can with both _____ open.

7. We moved from <u>house</u> to <u>house</u> until we had lived in five different _____.

8. He grew <u>inch</u> by <u>inch</u> until he had grown three _____.

9. One <u>box</u> was red and another <u>box</u> was blue, but all of the _____ had ribbons.

10. He hid behind one <u>bush</u> then ran to the _____ on the other side of the lawn.

Spell Check 12   Part II: Base Word + Inflection: Past Tense (Based on Sort 46)

Name _____

*Read each sentence carefully and look for the underlined word. Complete each sentence by changing the underlined word to the **past tense**. Write the **past tense** of the word in the blank provided.*

1. Her teacher told her to <u>ask</u> nicely so she _____ as nicely as she could.

2. It might <u>rain</u> again today. Last night it _____ two inches.

3. I hope it will <u>snow</u> tonight. Last year it _____ on Valentine's Day.

4. The snow will <u>melt</u> when the sun comes out. Last time it _____ before noon.

5. He can <u>jump</u> higher than anyone on the team. He _____ seven feet at the last meet.

6. She can really <u>yell</u> loudly. She _____ so much at the game that she lost her voice.

7. The girls won't <u>start</u> in the race this week. Last week they _____ before the gun went off.

8. The workers <u>pick</u> apples all fall. Last fall they _____ 2,000 barrels of apples.

9. They <u>load</u> the apples onto trucks. Last year they _____ 500 trucks.

10. Mrs. Smith <u>walks</u> every day. Last week she _____ 10 miles.

Unit X Homophones

NOTES FOR THE TEACHER

Background and Objectives

By now your students have encountered many homophones in the previous sorts and hopefully these words have been brought to life through group discussions and extension activities. Homophones are fun to study because of the way meaning is altered by a simple change in the vowel pattern.

This unit presents a homophone fest and at the same time reviews many of the common long-vowel patterns. Some of the words repeat from previous sorts but many new ones are added as well. We recommend that these words be sorted first by pairs that sound alike. Students will most likely know the meaning of at least one word in the pair, so it will be easy for them to learn the meaning of the other one by contrast. For example, students are apt to know the meaning of the word *pain*, but may not be as familiar with the meaning of *pane*. By discussing the meaning of the word *pane* in contrast to the other *pain*, students will easily associate the window with the CVCe spelling. Students will:

- Learn the spellings and meanings of one-syllable long-vowel homophones

Targeted Learners

These sorts are intended to be used at the end of the within word pattern stage when students have good mastery of the various spelling patterns and are already familiar with at least one word of the homophone pair.

Teaching Tips

Developing the meaning of the homophones is very important. Students can be asked to use dictionaries to look up the meaning of some words during the introductory sort. Ask students to choose homophones to illustrate or use in sentences as part of their weekly routines. They can choose some of their favorites or ones that they find hardest to remember. As students work with a partner to do a blind sort or no-peeking sort they will need to define the words for each other in order to sort them, so this gives them additional practice thinking about the meaning of the words. Any classroom display that you might have been keeping will explode with the numbers of homophones in this unit!

Homophone games are described in Chapter 6 of *WTW*. We especially like Homophone Rummy and Homophone Win Lose or Draw. Memory or Concentration works well also because it involves making matching pairs.

Literature Connection

Look for books that have fun with homophones. Our favorites include *The King Who Rained* and others by Fred Gwynne, as well as the Amelia Bedelia books by Peggy Parish.

SORTS 47 AND 48   LONG -*A* HOMOPHONES

(See page 133–134.) There are 49 words in these two related sorts but some of them have shown up in previous sorts. Most of the long-vowel patterns presented will be familiar, but the *ei* pattern has not been introduced previously and will be covered here. This is a good place because for nearly all of the words in which the long -*a* sound is spelled *ei*, there is a homophone (*eight-ate, rein-rain, weigh-way, sleigh-slay*). If you live in Maine add that word to the sort.

Demonstrate

You might combine both sorts and do all the words at once, introduce them over a 2-day period, or do one each week for a 2-week period. Sort 47 has only two patterns (*a-e* and *ai*) and these could be done first. Sort 48 introduces the *ei* pattern and adds *ay* and *ea* so these words may be harder to learn to spell. Begin by asking students to cut apart their words and pair up the homophones. Review the meaning of *homophones* if necessary—words that sound alike but are spelled differently and have different meanings. Once the pairs are together, have students tell you the word meanings they know and have them look up others in the dictionary as part of the group discussion. You can tell them the meanings of any they do not know as well. Have your students draw little pictures on the homophones they do not know so they can remember them. Once this is accomplished, have your students sort the homophones by vowel patterns. *There, their,* and *they're* will be oddballs because they have the long -*a* sound but no long -*a* patterns. These will need to be used in sentences in order to explore their meaning and usage. The final sort will look like this:

a-e	ai	ea	ay	ei	oddball
mane	main				there
pale	pail				their
made	maid				they're
male	mail				
ale	ail				
pane	pain				
plane	plain				
waste	waist				
sale	sail				
hare	hair				
maze	maize				
daze			days		
ate				eight	
			way	weigh	
wade				weighed	
	wait			weight	
			slay	sleigh	

vane	vain		vein
	rain		rein
			reign

stake		steak
brake		break
bare		bear
pare	pair	pear

After your students have completed Sort 48, ask them if any new patterns came up. Some students may say the *ei* pattern while others may volunteer *eigh*. Some discussion of the silent letters *gh* may help them to broaden their category to accept all of the *ei* words together.

As an **extension**, other homophones from previous sorts to add to games for review include *tale-tail, fare-fair, stair-stare*.

SORT 49   LONG -*E* HOMOPHONES

Demonstrate, Sort, Check, and Reflect

(See page 135.) Sort 49 focuses on homophones with the long -*e* patterns of *ee* and *ea*. Introduce this sort like the previous one by having students match the homophones and then talk about their meaning. Then sort them by pattern. Scene is one of the few long -*e* words with the CVCe pattern.

ee	*ea*	oddball
sees	seas	seize
seen		scene
sweet		suite
beet	beat	
meet	meat	
feet	feat	
flee	flea	
steel	steal	
cheep	cheap	
heel	heal	
need	knead	
creek	creak	
deer	dear	

Extend

Other homophones from previous sorts to add to games for review include *week-weak, here-hear, peace-piece, read-red,* and *lead-led*.

SORT 50   LONG -*I* AND LONG -*O* HOMOPHONES

(See page 136.) Sort 50 focuses on homophones with the long -*i* and long -*o* sounds and patterns. Introduce this sort like the previous ones by having students match the homophones and then talk about their meaning. Then sort them by sound and pattern.

i-e	igh	y	oa	o-e	ow	oddball
die		dye	loan	lone		
write	right		rose		rows	
time		thyme	groan		grown	
side	sighed			close		clothes
site	sight		board	bored		
	night					
	knight					
		by, buy, bye				
aisle						I'll

Extend

Homophones from previous sorts to add to games for review include *no-know, rode-road, load-lode, or-ore-oar, boar-bore, sore-soar, horse-hoarse, throne-thrown, wore-war;* and *poor-pour* could also be added.

SORT 47   Long -a Homophones

mane	pale	made
pain	plain	their
hair	main	pane
male	ail	mail
pail	maid	ale
plane	sale	waste
there	waist	sail
maze	hare	they're
maize		

SORT 48   More Long -*a* Homophones

days	ate	way
wade	bear	wait
slay	vain	brake
eight	daze	weighed
vein	weigh	reign
pair	sleigh	weight
stake	rain	steak
break	vane	bare
pare	rein	pear

SORT 49 Long -e Homophones

sees	sweet	beet
flee	feet	heal
steal	seas	cheap
need	suite	flea
beat	creek	scene
heel	seize	deer
steel	creak	cheep
meat	seen	meet
knead	feat	dear

SORT 50   Long -*i* and Long -*o* Homophones

die	loan	rose
by	write	dye
groan	board	side
rows	clothes	site
close	right	grown
night	sighed	buy
bored	sight	lone
aisle	knight	I'll
bye	thyme	time

Appendix

Headers for Long and Short Vowels

Short ă	Long ā	Short a
Long a	Short ĕ	Long ē
Short e	Long e	Short ĭ
Long ī	Short i	Long i
Short ŏ	Long ō	Short ŏ
Long ō	Short ŭ	Long ū
Short ŭ	Long ū	
oddball	*oddball*	*oddball*

Vowel Pattern Headers

oddball	oddball	oddball
_o_e	_u_e	_a_e
_i_e	_ake	_ack
_oke	_ock	_ike
_ick	_uke	_uck
_ook	_oo_	_oa_
_ai_	_ui_	_ee_
_ea_	_ay	_ew
_ue	_ow	_y

Less Common Vowel Pattern Headers and Complex Consonant Cluster Headers

_ild	_igh	_old
_ost	_ind	_air
_ear	_are	_ire
_ier	_eer	_oar
wor_	_ore	_ure
_oi_	_oy	_au_
_aw	_oo_	_al_
wa_	_dge	_ge

More Spelling Headers

kn_	wr_	gn_
scr_	str_	spr_
thr_	shr_	squ_
_ce	_ve	_se
_tch	_ch	

Blank Sort Template

Independent Word Study

Name _____ Date _____

Cut apart your words and sort them first. Then write your words below under a key word.

_____

_____

_____

_____

_____

_____

_____

_____

_____

_____

_____

What did you learn about words from this sort?

_____

_____

_____

On the back of this paper write the same key words you used above. Ask someone to shuffle your word cards and call them aloud as you write them into categories. Look at each word as soon as you write it. Correct it if needed.

Check off what you did and ask a parent to sign below.
_____ Sort the words again in the same categories you did in school.
_____ Write the words in categories as you copy the words.
_____ Do a no-peeking sort with someone at home.
_____ Write the words into categories as someone calls them aloud.
_____ Find more words in your reading that have the same sound and/or pattern. Add them to the categories on the back.
Signature of Parent _____

about*	43	blurt	29	cent	39	cough	34
above	43	board	28, 50	center	39	could*	32
across	43	boat	14	chain	13	couldn't	44
afraid	43	boil	31	chair	25	could've	44
again*	43	book*	12	chalk	34	count	35
age	41	bored	50	chance	40	crab	11
ago	43	bosses	45	change	41	crawl	33
aid	19	both*	23	charge	41	creak	49
aisle	50	bought	34	cheap	49	cream	18
alive	43	bounce	40	cheek	18	creek	49
almost	34	bowl	31	cheep	49	crew	21
along	43	box	14	cheer	26	crier	27
also	34	boxes	45	cheese	40	crook	32
aren't	44	boy*	31	chew	21	crop	11
around	43	brain	13	child	23	cross	33
ask	7	brake	48	choice	31	crow	24
asked	46	branch	42	choke	31	crunch	42
asleep	43	brave	19	choose	40	crust	15
ate	48	bread	17	chop	9	cry	22
away*	43	break	48	chose	14	cub	39
badge	41	breath	17	church	29	cube	6, 15
badges	45	bridge	41	churn	29	curb	29
bald	34	bright	22	circle	39	cure	29
bare	25, 48	broil	31	city	39	curl	29
beach	17, 42	broke	9	classes	45	curse	29
bear	25, 48	brook	32	claw	33	curve	29
beat	49	broom	15	clay	19	cute	10
beast	18	brought	34	clean	16	cycle	39
because*	43	brown	35	cleaned	46	dance	40
bee	6	brush	21	clear	26	dark	25
beet	49	build	15	clerk	26	dawn	33
become	43	bulge	41	cloak	31	day*	19
been*	16	bump	15	close	20, 50	days	48
before*	43	bumped	46	cloth	33	daze	48
began	43	burn	29	clothes	50	dead	17
begin	43	burst	29	cloud	35	deaf	18
behind	43	bushes	45	clown	35	dear*	26, 49
believe	43	buy	50	club	10	death	17
below	43	by*	50	clue	24	deer	26, 49
bench	42	bye	50	coach	20, 42	dew	21
beside	43	cage	41	coaches	45	die	50
between	43	calf	39	coal	20	dirt	27
beyond	43	calm	34	coast	18	dish	8
bike	6, 12	came*	7	coat	14	dishes	45
bind	24	camp	13	code	39	do*	21
bird	27	cane	6	coil	31	dodge	41
birth	27	cape	11	coin	31	doesn't	44
black*	13	card	39	cold	23	done	11
blame	13	care	25	come*	9	don't*	44
bleed	24	cart	39	cook	12	door	28
blew	21	catch	42	cool	32	down*	35
blind	23	caught	33	cone	6	draw	33
bloom	15	cause	33	corn	28	dread	18
blow	20	cease	39	cost	23	dream	17
blue	21	cell	39	couch	35	dressed	46

*High Frequency Words

sled	17	stalk	34	taught	33	trust	15
sleep	16	stall	34	taxes	45	truth	21
sleigh	48	stand	19	team	16	try	22
slide	24	stare	25, 47	tease	40	tube	10
slow	20	start	25	teeth	16	tune	10
small	34	started	46	term	26	turn	29
smoke	12	stay	19	that'll	44	turned	46
smooth	15	steak	48	their*	27, 47	twelve	40
snake	6	steal	49	there*	26, 47	twice	22
snap	7	steam	17	there's	44	twisted	46
sneak	24	steel	49	these*	11	use*	10
snooze	40	steep	24	they*	19	vain	48
snow	20	steer	26	they'll	44	vane	48
snowed	46	stew	21	they're	47	vault	33
soak	24	stitches	45	thin	8	vein	48
soap	14	stock	20	third	27	voice	31
soar	28	stole	31	this'll	44	vote	11
sock	12	stone	14	thorn	30	wade	48
soft	23	stood	32	those	9	waist	47
soil	31	stool	32	though	34	wait	18, 48
sold	24	stop	14	thought	34	waited	46
solve	40	store	28	thread	18	walk	34
some*	9	storm	28	threat	38	walked	46
song	33	stove	9	three*	18, 38	wand	34
soon*	32	straight	37	threw	38	want*	13
soot	32	strange	37	thrill	38	warm	
sore	28	strap	37	throat	18	wash	34
south	35	straw	33	throne	38	wasp	34
soy	31	stream	37	through	35, 38	waste	47
space	13	street	17	throw	20, 38	watch	34
speak	16	strength	37	thrown	38	wave	24
spear	26	stress	37	thumb	21	wax	11
speech	42	stretch	37	thyme	50	way*	24, 48
speeches	45	strict	37	tide	11	weak	16
spill	8	strike	12	time	50	wear	25
spoil	31	string	37	tire	27	web	16
spoke	12	stripe	37	toad	14	week	16
sponge	41	strong	37	toast	18	weigh	48
spoon	15	struck	37	told	23	weighed	48
spot	9	stuck	21	tone	24	weight	48
sprain	37	such*	10	took	12	were*	16, 29
spray	37	suit	15	tool	32	weren't	44
spread	37	suite	49	tooth	15	what*	7
spring	37	sure*	29	torch	42	what's	44
sprout	37	surf	29	tore	28	wheel	18
spur	30	surge	41	tough	35	when*	17
square	25, 38	swap	34	town	35	where*	25
squash	38	swat	34	toy	31	where's	44
squawk	38	sweep	16	trade	19	which*	11, 42
squeak	38	sweet	17, 49	trail	18	while*	8
squeeze	38	swim	8	train	13	whirl	27
squint	38	switch	42	tray	19	white*	22
squirm	38	tail	13, 47	tree	6	whole	31
squirt	38	take*	12	trees	17	who'll	44
squish	38	tale	13, 47	troop	32	who's	44
stage	41	talk	34	truck	12	whose	20
stair	25, 47	tape	6	true	21	why*	22
stake	48	taste	19	trunk	21	wife	11